# Cooking with Spices & Herbs

*By the Editors of Sunset Books
and Sunset Magazine*

*Lane Books · Menlo Park, California*

> For people who like to grow herbs in their
> own home gardens, a companion to this
> volume is the Sunset book, *How to Grow Herbs.*

*Edited by Judith A. Gaulke*

*Special Consultant: Annabel Post*

*Home Economics Editor, Sunset Magazine*

*Design: John Flack*

*Illustrations: Nancy Lawton*

*Cover: Left to right: fresh parsley, assorted red
    pepper flakes, jar of spicy mustard, whole cinnamon sticks,
    fennel seed, dill weed (hanging). Photograph by
    George Selland, Moss Photography.*

*Executive Editor, Sunset Books: David E. Clark*

Second Printing June 1974

*Copyright © 1974 Lane Magazine & Book Company, Menlo Park, California.
First Edition. World rights reserved.*

*Library of Congress No. 73-89587. Title No. 376-02681-2.
Lithographed in the United States.*

# Contents

## Special Features:

# An Introduction to
# Spices
# & Herbs

Confronting the spice rack at a supermarket can be very confusing, especially if you're a novice cook. With hundreds of seasonings to choose from, which ones will you find most useful? Is it better to rely on spice blends, such as fines herbes or seasoned pepper, or should you buy each spice or herb separately? You may even question whether they're worth the price.

Using spices and herbs with confidence is important. They are the key to more interesting menus; they can help the cook economize by enlivening simple, basic foods; and they are vital for enhancing diet dishes. But when many of their names and uses remain a mystery, it is difficult to choose wisely.

Confidence comes with familiarity. We propose to take the mystery out of cooking with spices and herbs. The descriptions starting on page 6 will introduce you to the tastes, aromas, and particular attributes distinguishing each spice and herb. This guide suggests the foods each enhances and gives specific suggestions for its use—whether it's a seasoning that can be used boldly or one better kept in the background.

You'll get to know any spice or herb best by cooking with it. We think a good way to begin is to use it in tested recipes. Once you learn to recognize its particular flavor and appreciate qualities it contributes to these dishes, you can begin to use it confidently and creatively with other foods.

The major part of this book contains easy-to-follow, thoroughly tested *Sunset* recipes. We hope they will help to expand your understanding and appreciation of herbs and spices while you are enjoying the delicious results.

## Storing seasonings at home

Heat, light, and moisture rob spices and herbs of their flavor. They keep best when stored in tightly closed containers in a cool, dark, dry place. Avoid locating that handsome spice rack right near the kitchen range, and be careful about opening a container over a steaming pot because the seasoning will cake.

Some spices and herbs are more perishable than others. In general, whole spices keep their flavors longest and finely ground spices for the shortest time. And if not stored properly, the bright green color of some herbs may fade and lose their flavoring effectiveness.

Any seasoning that has remained too long on your shelf should be discarded. Next time you might buy those you don't use very often in smaller amounts. Many spices and herbs are available in bulk. You can find them in small packets at supermarkets. Some specialty stores, health food stores, and delicatessens have an even wider selection. Often stores selling coffee and tea also deal in bulk spices.

## Using fresh herbs and spices

There are advantages to having fresh herbs right at hand. They can be picked when needed and their ultimate fresh flavors and aromas enjoyed immediately.

Small pots of growing herbs—chives, parsley, and thyme—can be found in nurseries as well as some supermarkets. Then you can grow them in an existing garden, on the patio, or lined along a kitchen window.

Herbs that grow well indoors can be transplanted to small containers or grown indoors from seeds. Herbs that will grow indoors are chervil, chives, marjoram, oregano, mint, rosemary, sage, and winter savory. Perennials, such as mint, rosemary, and thyme grow outdoors all year where winters are mild. (Directions for growing herbs indoors are found on page 29.)

Well stocked produce markets always have fresh parsley and often sell fresh basil, dill, and tarragon during their summer or early fall harvest seasons. Oriental or other specialty markets carry fresh ginger root and fresh coriander.

When substituting fresh herbs or spices for dried seasonings (or vice versa) in recipes not specifying equivalents, these guidelines are helpful. Consider first how finely chopped or pulverized the dried herbs are when measured. Then you can approximate the potency of ground or crushed dried herbs by finely chopping or mincing the fresh leaves and measuring about 3 or 4 times the amount of the dried volume. Or in other words, use only $\frac{1}{4}$ or $\frac{1}{3}$ as much dried herbs as fresh. But many variables can alter this formula. Because it tends to lose its flavor readily when dried and stored, mint, for example, may require nearly the same amount of dried leaves to equal the flavor of the fresh herb.

## Preserving fresh herbs

If you have an abundance of fresh herbs on hand in summer, you may want to preserve some for later use. They may be stored in several ways; the best method depends on the herb to be stored.

*Drying* is the easiest method of preserving herbs. You simply expose the leaves, flowers, or seeds to warm, dry air until the moisture is gone. The best time to harvest most herbs for drying is when the flowers first open. Ones having long stems—such as marjoram, sage, savory, mint, and rosemary—can be dried in bunches. Cut long branches and rinse in cool water, discarding any leaves that are dead or have lost their color. Tie the ends of the stems together into small bunches and hang them upside down in a warm dry room where they won't be exposed to direct sunlight. A warm, even temperature is best. Air should circulate freely around the drying herbs to absorb their moisture without destroying their oils, so don't hang them against a wall. If you dry herbs outside, bring them inside at night so the dew won't dampen them. To avoid collecting dust on the drying herbs, place each bunch inside a paper bag, gathering the top and tying the stem ends so that the herb leaves hang freely inside the bag. Cut out the bottom of the bag or punch air holes in the sides for ventilation.

After a week or two, the herbs should be crackly dry. Carefully remove the leaves without breaking them, then store in tightly sealed containers.

*Tray drying* is best for seeds, large-leafed herbs like basil, and short-tipped stems that are difficult to tie together for hanging. You can either remove the leaves from their stems or leave them attached, but spread only one layer of leaves on each tray. If you attempt to dry too many at once, air will not reach them evenly and they will take longer to cure. Screens or trays can be made to any size using window screening or cheesecloth for the drying deck.

Every few days stir or turn the leaves gently to assure even, thorough drying. It should take a week or so for them to dry completely, depending on the temperature and humidity. When the leaves are crisp and thoroughly dry, remove from racks.

Seeds can be spread on the trays or screens in a thin layer and dried in the same way as leaves. When the seeds are ready to shake loose from the dried seed capsules, carefully rub the capsules through your hands, blowing away the chaff.

*Microwave ovens* are a new and faster way to dry herbs. Rinse the herbs as for bunch or tray drying and shake off excess moisture. Put no more than 4 or 5 herb branches in the oven between two paper towels. Turn on oven for 2 to 3 minutes; remove from oven and place herbs on a rack. If not brittle and dry when removed from oven, re-peat microwave drying 30 seconds more. Then store as for regular dried herbs.

*Freezing* is a better way to preserve a few of the fresh, more tender herbs—basil, dill, chives, and tarragon. Simply wash, wipe dry, and freeze freshly picked herbs in small, airtight freezer bags, foil, or plastic wrap in amounts you might use at one time. Because frozen herbs will darken and become limp when thawed, add them directly to food you are cooking. Basil keeps best when made into pesto sauce—a paste of basil, oil, and Parmesan cheese—and frozen (directions on page 7).

## Guide to common spices and herbs

A precise definition of a "spice" and an "herb" is difficult. When referring generally to all aromatic plants used to season foods, however, the term "spices" is commonly used.

*Herbs* are the leaves of non-woody, low-growing shrubs or plants. They may be annuals, biennials, or perennials, and most grow in temperate climates. Aromatic seeds of herbs (such as caraway and poppy) are used as seasonings. Other plants (such as dill and coriander) produce both seeds and leaves, each with its distinctive flavor and culinary uses.

*Spices*, on the other hand, are generally derived from the bark, root, fruit, or berries of perennial plants and trees. Many are tropical in origin. For example, cinnamon is the bark of a tree, ginger the root of a tropical plant, nutmeg a fruit, and pepper a berry.

Other familiar products on your spice shelf are actually *blends* or mixtures of spices and herbs, such as curry, chile powder, seasoned salt, and pickling spice. Certain generally accepted ingredients go into these blends, but their exact formulas vary with each spice manufacturer.

The definitions that follow will hopefully broaden your knowledge of each spice and herb with basic information about the aroma, flavor, and other characteristics they can add to food.

## Allspice

Fruit of an evergreen tree, allspice is native to Jamaica, other islands of the West Indies, and Central America. The pea-sized allspice berry is picked from the tree while still green, then sundried until it turns dark, reddish brown and becomes small and hard. It is available both whole and ground. Whole allspice is one of the ingredients of the mixed pickling spice blend.

The flavor of allspice accounts for its name—it resembles a mixture of cloves, cinnamon, and nutmeg, with clove predominating. It combines well with other spices and is used in both sweet and savory dishes.

Use it in desserts—spice cakes and cookies; pumpkin, mincemeat, and other fruit pies; and in steamed puddings. It goes into sweet vegetable dishes—squash, sweet potatoes, carrots, eggplant, and tomatoes, as well as in tomato sauces and catsup. It is good with ham, in a variety of spicy meat dishes, and as an ingredient in many sausages. The whole spice is added to fish-poaching liquids and meat marinades.

## Anise

One of the oldest known herbs, anise was mentioned in ancient Egyptian records. It is an annual that is today cultivated for its small, greenish-gray seeds. Markets carry whole seeds, as well as anise extract and, occasionally, the ground seed. Anise oil is available in some drug stores. If you grow anise in an herb garden, you can use the small tender leaves, fresh or dry, to add to fruit or vegetable salads.

Both the seeds and leaves have a sweet, licorice-like flavor. In this respect, it resembles fennel. In some recipes, seeds of the two plants are interchangeable.

Anise seed is used in baking cookies, especially types such as German springerle and Italian twice-baked cookies. Scandinavian cooks use it in rye bread. It goes into coffee breads, cakes, even into apple pie. Spicy meat mixtures, sausage, poultry, cabbage slaw, and pickles all are enhanced by anise.

In addition to flavoring food, anise is the base for the liqueur anisette and also helps to flavor pernod.

## Basil or Sweet Basil

The popular herb basil is an annual that grows quickly to about 2 feet in warm climates. It has shining green leaves that are 1 to 2 inches long. If grown indoors, it requires sun and the stem tips should be pinched frequently so that it will grow bushy and full. You can buy bunches of fresh basil in some produce markets during the summer harvest season. The dried leaves are always available. Basil can also be purchased in pesto form (a paste of fresh basil, olive oil, and Parmesan cheese); look for it in the freezer case of your market or make your own, (see below).

Basil is a powerful herb with heady aroma and an adaptable taste. It is indispensable for Italian and other Mediterranean-style cookery, but it is native to the Near East and used in most countries around the world. Although it combines well with other herbs and is usually included in the fines herbes blend (see page 17), it is also one of the few herbs that can be allowed to really assert itself in certain dishes. It goes well with most vegetables, especially tomatoes, green beans, broccoli, eggplant, artichokes, peas, zucchini, and spinach. It's used in green salads, vegetable soups, egg dishes, pastas, and in many meat, fish, and poultry dishes. The flavor and green color of the dried leaves fade quickly, especially when exposed to heat and light. If you buy or harvest fresh basil, handle it gently because the leaves bruise easily, and they turn dark when dried. The best way to preserve a supply of the fresh herb is to freeze it—either in the form of pesto or simply blended with oil. To make pesto put 2 cups packed fresh basil leaves (washed and drained) in a blender jar; add 1 cup freshly grated Parmesan cheese and ½ cup olive oil. Turn motor on and off, whirling at high speed until all is coarsely puréed. Use immediately or freeze. Makes about 1½ cups. Or instead of making pesto, basil leaves may simply be whirled in a blender with just enough olive oil or salad oil to form a paste, then frozen. In this form it may be defrosted and used in salad dressings and to season vegetables and meats.

## Bay

The leaves of several varieties are sold as bay or bay laurel. Sweet bay or laurel is an evergreen shrub-tree native to the Mediterranean region having leaves 2 to 4 inches long, slightly serrated on the edges. The California bay laurel or Oregon myrtle, a much larger tree, has brighter green leaves and is more pungent in aroma; however, 90 percent of all bay used in the United States is of the Mediterranean variety because of its smoother, pleasantly full flavor. Bay leaves are available whole or cracked, rarely ground.

Use bay with care or its heavy flavor may overpower foods. Hearty meat and fish dishes such as stews and soups benefit from bay seasoning. The French always include it in a bouquet garni used to flavor the cooking broth for fish, game, poultry, and meats. A single leaf cooked in a terrine or meat loaf, or on baked fish, seasons it well. Use it, too, in liver paté, tomato soup, or aspic.

# Caraway

This biennial herb with lacy foliage resembling carrot is propagated for its seeds which ripen after the plant dies. Our commercial supply of the brown, crescent-shaped seeds comes principally from the Netherlands. It is sold as whole dried seed, occasionally as ground seed.

Caraway has a fresh clean taste that has the effect of lightening the flavor of such heavy foods as pork and sauerkraut. Hungarian cooks use it in goulash and liptauer cheese. Caraway's slight aroma of licorice is evident in a loaf of fresh caraway rye bread.

Other foods to season with caraway include cabbage and cucumber salads; such vegetables as carrots, green beans, and potatoes; and hearty meat dishes—oxtail stew, sausage, and spareribs. But it also has a sweetness in its character that is interesting with some fruits, especially apples, or with a pound cake.

# Cardamom

Although this spice is native to India, much of our supply now comes from Guatemala. The cardamom plant, a perennial belonging to the ginger family, produces green seed pods that are harvested by hand. They reach the grocery shelves usually as pithy, 3-sided, creamy white pods about the size of large peas with clusters of hard, dark brown seeds inside. Cardamom is also available ground without the pod.

Pungent, aromatic cardamom has an interesting flowery sweetness that is a little like ginger but considerably more subtle. It is used extensively in India where it goes into most curry dishes, as well as into sweets. It is an ingredient in curry powder.

Interestingly, it has been a favorite spice in Scandinavian countries since the early Vikings brought it home from Constantinople. Cardamom is used in all kinds of pastries, coffee cakes, and cookies, as well as in Swedish meatballs, pork, poultry, and fish. Try it instead of cinnamon with fruits—peaches, apples, and melon. It is often used with cabbage and other vegetables, and it is delicious with coffee and in spiced punches.

# Cayenne (see under Chiles, page 9)

# Celery

Most celery seed is not a product of cultivated celery but is the fruit of a wild celery called smallage. Its tiny brown seeds are sweetly aromatic, somewhat bitter. Both the whole and ground seeds are available.

The characteristic taste of fresh celery comes through in celery seed, so use it in combinations where you might add that vegetable, such as stews, with other vegetable dishes, in soups, and salads. It is one of the ingredients of pickling spice and goes into curry blends.

Use it for appetizers, in rolls, breads, and in poultry stuffings. It can season most meat, fish, and egg dishes but should always be used lightly so its powerful flavors won't dominate other food flavors.

# Chervil

The lacy, bright green leaves of chervil resemble parsley. It will grow readily in an herb garden. Though short-lived, this annual will reseed itself, if flowers are allowed to mature. It is readily available as dried leaves.

The pleasant aromatic flavor of chervil is more subtle than parsley. It also has spicy overtones and a slight flavor of licorice.

In France, where it is used far more extensively than in the United States, chervil is considered a blending herb, always part of the fines herbs combination. Because of its delicate nature, chervil can be used generously and in combination with most other herbs, helping to smooth their flavors. It is at its best in all kinds of salads. Cooking diminishes its flavor, so add it at the last minute to soups, sauces, egg and fish dishes. Use fresh chervil branches as garnish.

# Chiles

From two large and diverse species (known botanically as *capsicum frutescen* and *annuum*) come a remarkable number of seasonings and vegetables. They extend from fiery hot chiles that make cayenne and liquid hot pepper seasoning to the sweet mild chiles that make paprika, from tiny dried hot chiles and jalapenos to big sweet fresh bell peppers. They also include those middle-sized chiles—Fresnos, pimientos, California green chiles, and wax peppers—so indispensable to Mexican, Spanish, and Italian cooks who use them fresh, canned, pickled, or dried. Although sometimes called peppers, they are in no way related to the plant that gives us black and white pepper.

Of the many chiles, these are the major ones that are dried and used as spices:

**Paprika.** A number of sweet varieties of *capsicum annuum* are cultivated in Central and South America, Spain, Hungary, and the United States. Flavor and color are influenced by growing conditions and varieties. Spanish and American paprika are the brightest red color. Hungarian paprika has the fullest flavor without the harshness that is especially typical of Spanish paprika. Most cooks know paprika's value in adding bright red color to dishes, but Hungarians are masters at using it for flavor—goulash and liptauer cheese are examples.

**Chile Powder** (see Blends, page 17)

**Cayenne.** Several small species that produce very hot chiles are dried and processed for cayenne pepper. They vary in color from orange-red to deep red. Some of the very hottest come from Africa. Chiles don't have aromatic oil; their effect of heat is caused by a chemical reaction that stings the membranes of the mouth and nose. Be careful in handling hot peppers, for they can actually burn the skin or eyes. On the other hand, just a dash of cayenne can add zest to many dishes and bring out their natural flavors.

**Crushed red peppers.** Some of the hot chiles (called peperoni rosso) are not as hot as cayenne chiles but are dried and crushed for this seasoning. They are much used by Italian cooks—generously sprinkled on pizzas and in their sauces.

**Small dried hot chile peppers.** Possibly labeled small hot chiles, chile tepines, or chile pequins,

these are sold as dried whole chiles. The varieties differ somewhat in flavor, but all are fiery hot. Cracking open the chile and removing the seeds inside somewhat reduces the fire. They may be left whole in pickling spice. Sometimes the whole chile is cooked in a recipe, then removed before serving; other times, it is seeded and crushed to add to a dish. Use sparingly.

# Chives (see under Onion, page 13)

# Cinnamon

To make cinnamon sticks, the bark of an evergreen tree is peeled from the tree, rolled into quills and dried; or cinnamon is ground to make the popular sweet spice. The true cinnamon tree grows only in Ceylon, Madagascar, and the Seychelle Islands.

Delicate in flavor and color and preferred by Mexican cooks, true cinnamon accounts for only a small per cent of the world's supply. What most of the world prefers and calls cinnamon is actually the bark of a cassia tree, either Saigon cassia, Batavia or Korintji cassia from Indonesia, or cassia from the People's Republic of China. All have a strong, sweet spicy flavor and aroma.

The typical uses for cinnamon are so well known that they don't need to be enumerated. Some of its more subtle ways are in helping to season meats, especially lamb, pork, tongue, sausages, corned beef, chicken, and any meat cooked with fruit. It also enhances vegetables—carrots, squash, eggplant, and tomatoes.

# Cloves

Cultivated in Indonesia, Zanzibar, and Madagascar, cloves are the unopened flower buds of an evergreen tree. The familiar whole spice looks like a short nail. In fact, the name comes from "*clou*," the French word for nail. Cloves are available whole or ground.

Clove has a strong, pungent, almost hot flavor. It's the spiciest of the sweet spices—a little goes a long way in most foods. Heat releases extra pungency of whole cloves so fewer are needed in cooked foods than when added to an unheated one—marinade, for example. The uses of clove are wide ranging and most are quite familiar. More surprising are the warm flavor nuances achieved by blending a tiny bit of cloves with bay, cinnamon, ginger, or curry in spicy meat, fish, and poultry dishes and in chile sauce, chutney, and tomato sauces.

## Coriander

The fresh, green coriander plant looks like a bunch of parsley, and in much of the world it is used in this form as extensively as fresh parsley is here. The fresh herb is rapidly being discovered by cooks in the United States, especially those who enjoy trying ethnic dishes. Look for the bunches in produce markets, especially those catering to Mexican or Oriental cooks. It may be called cilantro in Mexican areas, Chinese parsley in Oriental areas. At least one spice company now sells the dried coriander (or cilantro) leaves.

The same plant produces coriander seed, which is sold whole or ground. The seeds have a warm taste that has been described as reminiscent of lemon and sage with a slightly bitter, musty quality.

The flavor of the fresh herb is unique and only slightly resembles ground coriander. Both the stems and leaves are highly aromatic; if you sprinkle them on a hot brothy soup, the headiness noticeably wafts up. It is not a flavor to use indiscriminately or timidly. It belongs with certain foods such as beans, corn, pork, or duck and with assertive spicy seasonings such as garlic, curry, or chile. You can experiment with it by trying classic dishes with origins in Mexico, South America, China, India, and Mediterranean countries.

Freshness is one dimension of the taste of this green herb; it can best be preserved at home by putting the stems in cool water, covering the container with a plastic bag, and storing in the refrigerator. For maximum flavor, chop just before use.

## Cumin

Native to the Mediterranean area, this small dried fruit of a low growing annual herb is called *comino* in many European countries, in Mexico, and in some foreign markets in the United States. The seed is available whole or ground.

Having a taste similar to caraway seed, cumin is a heady spice with a warm, slightly bitter taste.

Cumin has been known through the ages and in all parts of the world. Today, its uses vary by cuisine. It is much loved in Mexico, where it's an essential ingredient of chile powder. In India it goes into most curries and many condiments. In the Orient, as well as Spain, Portugal, Mediterranean, and Arab countries, it seasons all kinds of robust, spicy meat and vegetable dishes. The Dutch and Swiss use it principally to flavor cheese; the Germans use it in sauerkraut.

## Curry Powder

(see under Blends, page 17)

## Dill

All parts of this tall, graceful plant with feathery leaves carry the clean, fresh characteristics of dill and are useful seasonings. The mature plants with greenish-yellow flower heads are a familiar sight, standing in bunches in produce markets through late summer for the convenience of pickle makers. The lacy green leaves are dried, packaged, and sold as dill weed. Much of the dill seed we use, both whole and ground, is imported from India.

Fresh dill foliage has a rather delicate flavor and can be used generously in salads and with most vegetables, fish, and shellfish. (To Scandinavian cooks it's an essential seasoning for salmon, crayfish, cucumber salads, and especially new potatoes.)

Although you can snip the fresh leaves any time, the plant is at its peak flavor when the flowers are just opening. Use dill that is as fresh as possible for it loses flavor when dried. If possible, keep dill weed in the refrigerator or freeze a supply of the leaves from your summer garden.

The dill seed has more dominant flavor, with a sharp warm slightly bitter taste that resembles fennel. Use it in pickles, salad dressings, sauerkraut, and other strong vegetables, with meat, and in fish soups and stews.

# Fennel

Of the several varieties of this vegetable, common (or sweet) fennel is cultivated for the seed. The plant resembles dill, with flat clusters of yellow flowers that form at the end of the stems. Another variety, Florence fennel, is sold in markets as a vegetable called fennel, finocchio, or anise. Wild fennel is a plant that grows in fields familiarly in Mediterranean-type climates around the world.

Fennel seed is sold whole or ground. The feathery green tops on the vegetable fennel are also useful for seasoning.

The seed has an agreeable sweet taste with a slight flavor and aroma of licorice. It most resembles anise seed and is used in many of the same ways. Use it in breads, in spicy meat mixtures, sausages, and fish.

Feathery fennel leaves have a more delicate licorice flavor than the seed; try them in salads and soups, with vegetables, and with fish.

# Garlic (see under Onion, page 13)

# Ginger

Throughout history, the root of this semi-tropical plant has been one of the world's most important spices. It was one of the first Oriental spices known in Europe. Now ginger is cultivated extensively in Africa, India, China, Japan, and the West Indies. Jamaican ginger is considered to have the highest quality.

In addition to the familiar ground ginger, some spice companies package whole dry ginger; when soaked in cold water overnight (or until it rehydrates) it can be substituted for the fresh root. Oriental stores and many produce markets carry fresh ginger, indispensable for Oriental cooks. Crystallized and preserved ginger, considered confections, are also delicious seasonings for sweet dishes.

The clean, hot, spicy-sweet taste and rich pungent fragrance of ginger pleases most palates. It is the cook's friend because it has powers of both smoothing some flavors and accenting others, and it contributes a quality of freshness to foods seasoned.

Heat releases ginger's powerful flavor. Just 1 or 2 thin slices on fish while it steams or inside roasting chicken flavor the whole. It is best to grate fresh ginger when adding it to uncooked marinades. A good way to keep a supply of fresh ginger on hand is to freeze a well-wrapped root; grate or cut off what you need without defrosting.

# Horseradish

The horseradish plant belongs to the mustard family. It's a hearty perennial that produces long, thick roots resembling parsnips. Horseradish roots are ground and blended with vinegar and salt to make the familiar condiment, prepared horseradish. The root is also available in a dehydrated granular form. Produce markets sometimes sell fresh horseradish root that can be used to make your own prepared horseradish (directions to make your own are on page 42) or used freshly grated.

Horseradish has a hot, pungent flavor that has also a cooling effect on the taste buds. Blended into whipped cream, it makes a delicious sauce to serve with ham, roast beef, tongue, corned beef, and green vegetables, such as broccoli. Horseradish is a delicious flavor with fish and shellfish, relishes, appetizer dips, and salad dressings.

# Mace (see under Nutmeg, page 12)

# Marjoram

Sweet marjoram, an herb with light gray-green leaves native to the Mediterranean regions, is now widely cultivated around the world. It grows in low bushes; though a perennial, often it is grown as an annual in cool climates. It can be cultivated successfully in pots indoors. Botanically, marjoram is closely related to oregano; both are of the mint family. Their flavors (rather spicy and slightly bitter) are similar, but marjoram is sweeter and more mild than oregano. Marjoram is available as whole or crushed leaves and ground.

Although this herb can be sprinkled quite freely over a robust dish like pizza, anyone learning to cook with marjoram is wise to use it rather sparingly at first, especially with a delicate meat like veal. Its Mediterranean heritage suggests some of its best uses, for it does well in a wide variety of meat, game, fowl, and fish recipes from Italy, France, or Greece. Try it also in stuffings, with eggs, and especially with eggplant, summer squash, tomatoes, and mushrooms. It is usually included in a bouquet garni and among Italian seasoning blends.

# Mint

Coming in many varieties with a fascinating range of flavors and fragrance, mint is readily available to home gardeners. Some mints, such as apple and orange types, have fruity overtones. The most common garden mint is spearmint. Both spearmint and peppermint are widely used all over the world.

Of the two most common mints, peppermint has the sharper, more pungent flavor; it goes into candy and toothpaste. More delicate spearmint is used for mint jelly and sauces. All the mints have a refreshingly cool, sweet flavor.

Spice companies package dry mint leaves; fresh mint is available in some produce markets. It is also available as liquid mint extract.

Mint's virtues as a garnish and flavoring for beverages are well known. In addition, it is good with beef, veal, and fish, as well as with lamb, and in both fruit and vegetable salads. Vegetables having an affinity for mint include beans, carrots, eggplant, peas, potatoes, and spinach. Because cooking diminishes mint's flavor, add it shortly before serving. Crush the dried leaves just before adding them to a dish.

# Mustard

Small but mighty mustard seeds come from a plant that grows wild in much of the world. Of the many varieties known, only two are widely cultivated. Black mustard produces dark, reddish-brown seeds that are the most potent in flavor. White mustard, with pale yellow seeds, is milder. Mustard seeds are dried, ground, and sifted to produce dry or powdered mustard (sometimes called mustard flour); most packaged mustards are blends of seeds of different varieties so may be "mild" or "hot," depending on the seeds used.

Prepared mustards are made by grinding mustard seed or blending powdered mustard to a paste with vinegar and other seasonings (a little turmeric adds the bright yellow color in most mustards). The "hot" mustard that Chinese restaurants serve as a condiment is dry mustard blended to a thick paste with just a little liquid.

Mustard seed is an ingredient in pickling spice. It adds an interesting crunchy bite when used with corned beef, sauerkraut, chutney, or salad dressings. In its numerous varieties, mustard is used to season just about any savory dish.

If you would like to make your own flavorful mustards, we have included some intriguing homemade recipes on page 45. All are easy to prepare and delicious to use.

# Nutmeg

Both mace and nutmeg spices grow on the lovely tropical nutmeg tree. The red outer lacy skin (or aril) covering the nutmeg seed or nut is mace. In harvesting, the mace is removed and dried, then the nutmeg can be used whole. For the freshest flavor, buy dried whole nutmegs and grate what you need. They are also available ground. Mace is available whole in flat, branched, irregular pieces as well as in ground form.

The two spices are quite similar in flavor and can often be used interchangeably in cooking. Although both mace and nutmeg have strong, spicy sweet flavors, mace is more intense and pungent than nutmeg. Mace is used when brown specks of nutmeg are not desired. Both mace and nutmeg are often used in combination with cinnamon, allspice, cloves, or ginger for all kinds of sweet spicy baking, to spice fruit, and with custards. Used judiciously, nutmeg can add a subtle, exciting flavor lift to meats and cream sauces for chicken or veal. Before serving vegetables next time, grate a little over the top.

# Onion

The vast number of onion varieties and their cousins—the chives, leeks, shallots, and garlics—offers cooks a wide range of flavors. The onion family has a remarkable affinity for almost all meats, vegetables, fish, poultry, eggs, and cheese. Some are mild, others potent. Fortunately, they are available year around and in many convenient forms—fresh, dehydrated, frozen, in seasoning salts, and in spice blends.

**Onions.** In general, onions that grow during short winter days in mild climates are soft, sweet, and mild. Those that grow during summer and are harvested in fall are firm and strong in flavor.

Because they have less moisture content, they store well. The flavor substance in onions is a volatile oil. Boiling onions in water minimizes the flavor. Sautéing them slowly in butter or oil converts all of the harsh raw flavor to mellow sweetness. Convenient onion products include instant minced onion (plain and toasted), onion powder, and onion salt.

**Shallots.** These are small, brown skinned bulbs that form in cloves like garlic and have pinkish-white inner skins. *Échalotes* is the French name for this elegant member of the onion family. But shallots are more delicate than onions, with a distinctive sweet flavor. They are available as dry whole bulbs in produce markets and in the freeze-dried form.

**Garlic.** Two kinds of garlic are available; one is a small white-skinned bulb; the other is larger with red or purple skin. Both form in bulb clusters containing individual cloves and are similar in flavor.

The aroma from its volatile oils gives garlic its pungency; that is the reason a cut clove swished around the salad bowl seasons a salad so effectively. When you cook with garlic, be careful not to overbrown it, for it burns easily and develops a bitter taste. Garlic is widely available also in dehydrated forms—garlic powder, salt, chips, purée, and in seasoning blends.

**Chives.** This meekest of all onions is used as a fresh herb. When used fresh, the tender long tubular leaves lend a delicate onion flavor to salads, soups, and vegetables. Easy to grow in pots, they are sometimes sold as living plants in produce markets so cooks can snip off the leaves as they are needed. They are also available freeze-dried and frozen.

# Oregano

Another name for oregano (closely related to sweet marjoram) is wild marjoram. Available as dried whole leaves, oregano is an attractive perennial shrub that grows to about 2 or 2½ feet. It makes a good container plant. Most widely used and preferred in the West is the Mexican variety. This type is essential as an ingredient in chile powder.

Oregano is stronger and heavier in aroma and flavor than marjoram. Many know it as the seasoning on pizza. Italian, Greek, and Mexican cooks often use it liberally in spaghetti sauce, grilled meats, and hearty stews. It goes well with most Mediterranean vegetables, especially tomatoes, peppers, and beans. Oregano's potent flavor can

easily overpower the flavors of other food, so it's best to use it sparingly at first.

# Paprika (see under Chiles, page 9)

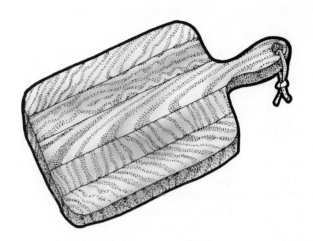

# Parsley

The most common variety, French parsley, has dark, curly green leaves. Italian parsley, with plain, flat leaves, is preferred by some cooks because it has a fuller, yet smoother and sweeter flavor than the curly variety. In addition to the bunches of fresh parsley from the market, the dehydrated leaves, called parsley flakes, are available.

The bright green leaves of parsley have a sharp, peppery taste. The parsley stems actually carry more of the flavor than the leaves.

Parsley's uses as a garnish, as salad greens, and as seasoning are well known. It blends well with other seasonings or stands alone and can be used generously or lightly. It goes into most herb blends, adding a fresh, clean taste to meats, soups, stews, and vegetable dishes.

# Pepper

Both black and white pepper come from tiny round berries, the fruit of a climber perennial vine native to the East Indies. Pepper was so valuable in medieval times that, like gold, it was used as a medium of exchange. And perhaps more than any other spice, pepper lured early explorers to find shorter routes to the Indies. Pepper takes on the name of its origin—Java, Lampong, Malabar, Sarawak, and Tellicherry—areas all rich in pepper today.

*(Continued on next page)*

Pepper berries grow in clusters like grapes; they are picked before ripe and dried. When dried, the pepper turns dark and wrinkled—this is the familiar whole black pepper.

To produce *white pepper*, the pepper berry is allowed to ripen before picked. Then the dark outer coating is removed from the pepper berry, exposing a creamy white core.

White pepper shares the same warm pungent fragrance and flavor as black but is milder and sweeter. It can be used sparingly to add a subtle spicy flavor to delicately flavored foods or applied more generously. Some fish and egg dishes take well to it, and it is widely used in creamy sauces and soups in which black specks of pepper might detract from the appearance of the dish.

In its whole form, pepper can be stored for many years without losing its aroma and potency. A pepper grinder provides freshly ground pepper whenever needed. Pepper is available whole, cracked, and coarsely or finely ground. White pepper comes whole or ground.

*Green peppercorns* (*poivre vert*) are also available. They are tender, immature forms of whole black pepper, packed in brine, and resemble small capers. They are available in jars or cans in specialty food stores. Crushed slightly and usually mixed with butter, they impart a fresh, mild, peppery flavor to steak, duck, or roasts.

# Poppy Seed

One particular species of poppy is cultivated for the tiny, slate-blue seeds used in cooking. Although it probably originated in Asia, poppy seed is now cultivated in many countries of the world. Some of the best comes from the Netherlands. It is available as whole seed.

Heat releases the rich, nut-like flavor of poppy seeds. They add a crunchy texture and interesting flavor to breads and rolls, cookies, pie crust, or cake. Hungarian cooks make fillings for cakes and pastries by grinding large quantities of poppy seed into a paste sweetened with sugar or honey. Poppy seed can be heated in butter, then used

to season vegetables (peas, rutabaga, or turnips). Or you can toast the seeds in a dry frying pan to add to cheese spreads, canapes, and fruit or vegetable salads.

# Rosemary

These aromatic herbs are hearty perennials that grow 2 to 6 feet high, depending on the variety. All have narrow leaves that look like fine, short pine needles. Rosemary hails from the Mediterranean. It is often used in garden landscaping where winters are mild, but it also grows well in containers and can be brought indoors for the winter. So cooks everywhere can have a supply of the fresh herb on hand. The dried whole leaves are also available.

Rosemary has a bold flavor often described as piney and slightly resinous with a sweet scent. It is very much at home around the barbecue. Poke some of the needles into a leg of lamb, inside poultry, or use it in meat marinades and bastes. Some chefs burn rosemary sprigs or leaves in the barbecue coals to add its flavor to meats, or tie rosemary sprigs together to use as a basting brush. Use it in stuffings for poultry or fish. It's tasty with pea soup, in savory breads, in stews, and with vegetables—beans, peas, spinach, and zucchini.

# Saffron

Unquestionably the most expensive spice in the world, saffron comes from the dried stigmas of the little purple saffron crocus. The reason it is so expensive is that it takes thousands of hand-picked flower stigmas to make a pound of saffron. Most saffron now comes from Spain, but it is native to both southern Europe and Asia. It's available ground or in dried whole "threads" or stigmas.

Fortunately, saffron has a mighty powerful flavor—a little goes a long way. Recipes often call for as little as $\frac{1}{32}$ of a teaspoon. It has a unique, earthy flavor that is pleasantly bitter. Spanish cooks use it in paella and many other poultry, seafood, and rice dishes. Scandinavians make sweet saffron buns and breads from it. It is also a popular seasoning in South America and most of the Mediterranean countries.

# Sage

Of the many species of sage, only one, common garden sage, is used extensively for cooking.

(Don't confuse it with the American sage brush.) It is a perennial shrub that grows 2 to 3 feet high and has oval, gray-green leaves 1 to 2 inches long. Native to Dalmatia, Yugoslavia, which supplies much of the world, sage is also now widely cultivated in California and other western states. The dried sage leaves are available whole, rubbed (crushed), or ground.

Sage is easily recognized as the predominant flavor in poultry seasonings; think of your Thanksgiving turkey. It's a fragrant herb with a warm, slightly bitter taste. In spite of its assertive flavor, sage is a versatile seasoning, delicious with pork, lamb, veal, game, duck, and richly flavored fish, sausages, and meat stuffing. The Swiss flavor cheese with sage. You might mix it into cheese spreads, add it to fish chowders, or use it with vegetables, especially lima beans, onions, tomatoes, and eggplant.

## Savory

There are two savories: summer savory—an annual that grows quickly to about 18 inches in height; and winter savory—an attractive perennial that is a spreading compact plant. Both make good container plants.

The savories have warm peppery flavor with resinous overtones and grassy fragrance. Summer savory, though, has a sweeter, more delicate flavor and is generally preferred for cooking. It is available as whole leaves and ground.

Native to southern Europe, savory is now grown throughout Europe and the United States. It goes with Mediterranean-style of cooking and blends well with other herbs in a bouquet garni or fines herbs blend. It is also an ingredient in poultry seasoning.

Savory flavors enhance all kinds of dry legumes, green beans, and other vegetables. Used sparingly, it can season fish, eggs, and meat dishes.

## Sesame Seed

This important seed is the dried fruit of a tropical annual that grows to about 2 feet tall. It is cultivated extensively in China, Africa, India, and South and Central America. The tiny, smooth, creamy-white hulled seeds are available whole or toasted. Oriental stores also sell sesame oil. When ground into a paste, it is called tahini; in this form it is widely used in Middle Eastern delicacies. It is also the basis of the Jewish candy, halvah.

Heating or toasting is needed to release the rich, nut-like flavor of sesame. One cannot think of many foods that are not receptive to the flavor and crunch of sesame. Put the toasted seeds over meat, fish, poultry, or Chinese meat and vegetable combinations. Heat sesame seeds in butter to season vegetables. Use them like chopped nuts in or on top of breads, rolls, cakes, and cookies. Sprinkle them into salads and soups.

## Shallots (see under Onion, page 13)

## Tarragon

French tarragon, the herb grown for culinary use, is a woody, spreading perennial with slender, dark green leaves. It is propagated by root cuttings and does not produce seeds. If you find tarragon seeds, they come from another variety, Russian tarragon, that does not have the same characteristic tarragon flavor. Fresh tarragon is occasionally sold in vegetable markets. The dried leaves are always available.

The flavor of tarragon is uniquely spicy, sharp, and aromatic, with strong overtones of licorice and mint. Cooks don't all agree on the uses of tarragon: some apply it generously, letting its distinctive flavor sing out; others use it more sparingly to keep the flavor subtle. Cooks agree, though, that tarragon is best for dishes in which it can be the dominant flavoring. French cooks are masters with tarragon; their word for it, *estragen*, appears often on French menus. It's an essential ingredient for bearnaise sauce, served with asparagus and other vegetables, and eggs. Tarragon vinegar often comes with a sprig of tarragon in it for flavor. It is excellent in green salads. The fresh or dried leaves are good with chicken, fish, shellfish, lamb, and veal.

The dry herb loses flavor quite readily. To preserve fresh tarragon, freeze the sprigs airtight in plastic bags or blend with salad oil into a paste to freeze in small, rigid containers.

## Thyme

In addition to common thyme, one can grow other varieties with some delightfully different flavors. Lemon thyme, with its fragrant lemon aroma, is especially interesting in salads and with seafood. Thyme is a bushy, low growing perennial with oval gray-green leaves. The dry leaves are available whole and ground.

Thyme is a strong flavored herb with heavy, spicy aroma and pungent clove-like taste. It needs to be used sparingly but is a versatile herb that blends well with other herbs. It flavors poultry seasoning and many other herb blends. Benedictine liqueur is flavored with thyme. It does well in creamy soups and fish chowders and in all kinds of meat, fish, game, and poultry dishes. Vegetables that are enhanced by thyme include onions, carrots, beets, mushrooms, beans, potatoes, and tomatoes.

## Turmeric

Turmeric is the root of a tropical plant in the ginger family. Native to China and Indonesia, turmeric is now cultivated principally in India, Haiti, and Jamaica. Available ground and occasionally as whole dried root, it is best known as an ingredient in curry powder.

Turmeric, with its bitter-sweet flavor, resembles ginger. Unlike ginger, though, it has a slightly musty aroma and a brilliant yellow color. Just like saffron, a little turmeric adds rich golden color to cooked dishes or baked goods.

Turmeric is used most extensively in Indian cookery, flavoring all kinds of curries, condiments, and rice dishes. It is an ingredient in pickles and relishes. Used sparingly, it can give a new flavor and golden color to eggs, salad dressings, meat, fish, poultry, and rice dishes.

## Vanilla

After it blooms, an exotic orchid plant bears a cluster of long green pods called vanilla beans. Native to Mexico, history dates it long before the Aztecs, but it was introduced to the rest of the world when Cortez discovered it in the palace of Montezuma. Some of the finest vanilla is still produced in Mexico; however, the major production of beans today comes from Madagascar.

The green vanilla bean is harvested, cured, and dried before it turns a dark, chocolate color and develops its characteristic fragrance and sweet flavor. The painstaking process takes nearly 6 months and can be compared to producing a fine wine. The flavor is extracted from the bean by "percolating" it in huge vats with alcohol to make pure vanilla extract. (Imitation vanilla extract is artificial. It is a mixture of color and synthetic flavors, mainly vanillin.)

The sweet, fruity flavor and fragrance of vanilla enhances almost any dessert or fruit. Vanilla and chocolate always go well together. When used in small quantities, so its flavor isn't evident, vanilla has the effect of smoothing other flavors. It makes sugar seem sweeter. Bury a whole vanilla bean in a container of sugar to make vanilla sugar.

# TEN POPULAR BLENDS

## Chile Powder

The United States can claim chile powder as its own. Developed close to the southwestern border about 100 years ago, it has a strong Mexican influence. A ground blend, chile may be based on a combination of spices and herbs: cumin, coriander, chile peppers, garlic, cloves, paprika, salt, oregano, black pepper, and turmeric are typical ones used. The combination produces a taste and aroma that is hot, spicy, and slightly sweet, and sometimes very peppery.

## Chinese Five-Spice

The Chinese often blend several favorite spices together to flavor foods. The five major spices used are cloves, fennel, licorice root, cinnamon, and star anise (a seasoning growing only in China). Chinese five-spice is available as a ground blend in Oriental stores and many supermarkets. You can approximate the flavor by combining equal parts of ground cloves, anise, fennel, licorice root, and cinnamon.

## Curry Powder

Carefully compounded blendings of many spices make up curry powder. The blend varies considerably throughout the world, but it is usually a combination of six or more of the following spices and herbs: cumin, coriander, turmeric, ginger, pepper, dill, mace, cardamom, and cloves. Together, they give the characteristic sweet-hot curry flavor and aroma.

## Fines Herbes

Typically used in French cooking, fines herbes is usually a combination of finely minced fresh or dried parsley, chervil, tarragon, and chives mixed until well blended.

## Italian Herb Seasoning

The characteristic flavoring of Italian cooking comes from adding such seasonings as oregano, basil, red chile pepper, rosemary, and garlic. These are combined in one blend to accomplish the typical Italian seasoning.

## Pickling Spice

This blend is used for pickling and preserving meats and to season vegetables, relishes, and sauces. It is a mixture of whole spices, usually including mustard seed, bay leaves, black and white whole peppers, dill seed, red chile peppers, ginger, cinnamon, mace, allspice, coriander seed, and sometimes other spices.

## Poultry Seasoning

A ground blend of sage, thyme, marjoram, savory, and sometimes rosemary and other spices make up this seasoning, adding a characteristic flavoring to poultry.

## Pumpkin Pie Spice

The spices usually equated with pumpkin pie are joined in this ground blend: cinnamon, cloves, and ginger.

## Seasoned Salt and Seasoned Pepper

Spices and herbs are mixed with either salt or pepper, creating many all-purpose seasonings. They implement meats, poultry, fish, vegetable dishes, and can be used to test the imagination.

# Appetizers

*Ideas for Spicy Starters*

## HELPFUL HINTS

For easy finger sandwiches, spread thinly sliced pumpernickel bread with butter and cover with thin, overlapping, unpeeled slices of cucumber. Sprinkle with salt and dill weed. Or, trim crust of thinly sliced rye bread, spread with soft cream cheese and top with finely chopped parsley or chives, then cut in half.

Decorate and flavor a simple block of cream cheese by patting fresh or dried rosemary leaves into all its surfaces. Wrap and refrigerate 1 to 2 days. Unwrap and serve on a board with salted crackers.

As a switch from salted peanuts, try chile almonds. Put about 1 pound unblanched almonds in a frying pan with 1 tablespoon chile powder, 1 large clove crushed garlic, and ¼ cup butter. Stir over medium heat until crisp and lightly browned. Remove garlic and sprinkle with salt to taste.

Marinate 1 pound mushrooms (sliced lengthwise) in ¾ cup olive oil, 3 tablespoons tarragon vinegar, ½ teaspoon salt, a dash pepper, 2 teaspoons minced parsley, and ½ teaspoon minced fresh or dried tarragon. Let stand at room temperature for about 5 hours, then serve with picks.

To save time when making canapés, have your bakery slice loaves of bread lengthwise. You merely trim away crusts, then spread with soft butter and your choice of filling. Garnish the edges with a half-inch-wide border of finely chopped parsley, if you wish. Just before serving, cut across into finger-shaped individual canapés.

A quick dip for raw vegetables can be made by blending 2 cups prepared chive sour cream dressing with 1 teaspoon caraway seed and 2 teaspoons instant minced onion. Season with salt and pepper and chill several hours before serving.

## Curried Crab Spread

You can serve this curried crab in a bowl to spread on shredded wheat wafers or Melba toast. Or toast one side of small French bread slices or halved firm white bread slices with crusts removed; spread untoasted side with crab mixture, then top each with a thin slice of good melting cheese such as Swiss or jack. Set under broiler just to melt the cheese.

About 1 cup crab meat (fresh, frozen, or canned)
2 tablespoons fresh minced parsley (or 2 teaspoons dried parsley)
1 tablespoon finely minced onion (or 1 teaspoon instant minced onion)
3 tablespoons mayonnaise
¼ teaspoon curry powder
1 tablespoon lemon juice

Combine the crab meat with the parsley, onion, mayonnaise, curry powder, and lemon juice in a bowl; chill for 15 minutes. (If you use dehydrated parsley and onion, cover and refrigerate mixture at least 1 hour for flavors to mellow.) Makes about 1¼ cups spread.

## Cheese-Caraway Appetizers

Made in the same manner as refrigerator cookies, these tender cheese pastries are convenient to use. Refrigerate the rich dough shaped in a log, then simply slice, bake, and serve.

¾ cup butter or margarine
½ cup shredded sharp Cheddar cheese
½ cup crumbled blue-veined cheese
2 cups regular all-purpose flour (unsifted)
1½ teaspoons caraway seed
1 clove garlic, minced or mashed
2 tablespoons chopped chives (fresh, frozen, or freeze-dried)

With an electric mixer or wooden spoon, beat the butter, Cheddar cheese, and blue-veined cheese until smoothly blended. Stir in flour, caraway, garlic, and chives. Shape mixture into a log about 20 inches long and about 1¼ inches in diameter; wrap in waxed paper and chill until firm. (Wrap airtight to freeze.) To bake, cut off ¼-inch-thick slices of dough and place slightly apart on ungreased baking sheets. Bake in a 375° oven for 10 to 12 minutes or until lightly browned around edges. Serve warm or cooled. Makes about 7 dozen wafers.

## Almond Shrimp

These shrimp are a good choice when you plan an all-appetizer party.

½ cup (¼ lb.) butter or margarine
3 cloves garlic, minced or mashed
½ cup sliced almonds
2 pounds medium-sized shelled shrimp, cleaned and deveined
½ cup chopped parsley
Lemon wedges

Melt the butter in a wide frying pan. Add the garlic and almonds. Stir over medium heat until almonds are lightly toasted. Add shrimp; keep turning until meat is opaque (cut one to test); turn for about 5 minutes. Stir in the parsley. Transfer to a serving dish or warming tray. Accompany with lemon wedges. Makes 8 servings.

## Vegetables with Creamy Dill Dip

Chill the sauce at least 2 hours to allow flavors to blend, then serve with a variety of raw vegetables.

1 cup sour cream
¼ cup mayonnaise
1¼ teaspoons celery salt
1 tablespoon dill weed
1½ teaspoons dried parsley flakes
¼ teaspoon onion powder
1 clove garlic, minced or mashed
½ teaspoon prepared horseradish
Raw carrot or celery sticks, cauliflower pieces, cherry tomatoes

Combine the sour cream, mayonnaise, celery salt, dill weed, parsley flakes, onion powder, garlic, and horseradish in a bowl. Cover and chill at least 2 hours. Serve with carrot or celery sticks, cauliflower pieces, or cherry tomatoes for dipping. Makes about 1¼ cups dip.

## Spiced Liptauer Dip

Liptauer is the name of a soft cheese that was originally made by Hungarian villagers; now the word commonly refers to cheeses spiced with paprika and other zesty seasonings. Serve with rye bread slices or raw vegetables.

1¼ cups large curd cottage cheese
3 tablespoons finely sliced green onions
1½ tablespoons capers, drained and finely chopped
4 canned anchovy fillets, finely chopped
1 clove garlic, minced or mashed
1 teaspoon salt
½ teaspoon pepper
¾ teaspoon dry mustard
1 tablespoon paprika
2 packages (3 oz. each) cream cheese, at room temperature
½ cup (¼ lb.) soft butter or margarine
½ cup sour cream
1½ tablespoons caraway seed

In the small bowl of your electric mixer, combine the cottage cheese, onions, capers, anchovy, garlic, salt, pepper, mustard, and paprika. Beat at medium-high speed for 5 minutes or until curds are cut very fine. Beat in the cream cheese and butter, scraping bowl sides 2 or 3 times. Stir in sour cream and caraway until blended. Cover and refrigerate overnight or up to a week. Serve in a small bowl or crock. Makes 3 cups dip.

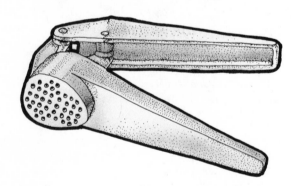

## Garlic Cheese Dip

Two favorite flavors, garlic and blue cheese, combine in this easily prepared dip. Serve with crisp vegetables or chips.

2 ounces blue cheese
1 cup mayonnaise
1 teaspoon instant minced onion
½ teaspoon Worcestershire
1¼ teaspoons garlic powder
Minced parsley

In a small bowl, mash blue cheese well with a fork. Stir in the mayonnaise, instant onion, Worcestershire, and garlic powder until well blended. Cover and chill until time to serve, then sprinkle with parsley. Makes about 1¼ cups dip.

## Parsley Cheese Ball

A green parsley coat decorates this flavorful cheese ball. Serve with crackers or apple slices.

1 package (8 oz.) cream cheese
3 cups (about 12 oz.) shredded sharp Cheddar cheese
2 tablespoons chopped green pepper
2 tablespoons finely chopped green onion
2 teaspoons Worcestershire
1 teaspoon each lemon juice and prepared mustard
Dash cayenne
⅛ teaspoon salt
About 1 cup chopped parsley
Assorted crackers or apple slices

Allow the cream cheese and Cheddar cheese to come to room temperature. In an electric mixer bowl beat the cheeses together until light and fluffy. Stir in the green pepper, onion, Worcestershire, lemon juice, mustard, cayenne, and salt. Cover and chill until firm enough to handle (about 2 hours).

Using your hands, shape the cheese mixture into a round ball; roll in chopped parsley to completely coat the ball. Wrap well and refrigerate overnight or as long as 5 days.

To serve, allow the cheese ball to stand at room temperature for about 30 minutes. Place on a tray and surround with crackers or apple slices. Makes 1 ball about 5 inches in diameter.

## Cardamom Crisps

Flour tortillas make crisp, tasty bases for these hot appetizers.

3 tablespoons soft butter or margarine
¼ teaspoon ground cardamom
4 flour tortillas

Blend the butter or margarine with the cardamom until smooth. Spread the tortillas with the butter mixture; cut into quarters. Bake on an ungreased baking sheet in a 400° oven for about 8 minutes or until crisp and golden. Serve hot. Makes 16 appetizers.

## Herring with Tomato-Mustard Sauce

Prepared herring from the refrigerated sections of supermarkets is the shortcut for this Scandinavian-style appetizer.

¾ cup tomato-based chile sauce
½ teaspoon mustard seed
¼ teaspoon dry mustard
¼ lemon (including peel), thinly sliced
½ teaspoon prepared horseradish
2 jars (6 to 8 oz. each) spiced cut herring
    Crisp lettuce leaves (optional)
    Buttered slices firm-textured rye or
        pumpernickel bread (optional)

In a small saucepan combine chile sauce, mustard seed, dry mustard, lemon, and horseradish; bring to a boil, stirring. Remove sauce from heat and blend in the herring. Cover and chill for at least 4 hours before serving (or store in the refrigerator up to one week).

They are easiest to eat with a knife and fork, but you can present them in several ways: spoon unadorned onto small plates, spoon into crisp lettuce leaves, or mound on buttered slices of firm-textured rye or pumpernickel bread. Makes about 2 cups.

## Teriyaki Tidbits

You can mix up your own Teriyaki Sauce, marinate the meats early in the day, and broil them just before serving to your gathering.

1 pound boneless meats, such as chicken,
    beefsteak, or chicken or beef liver
    Teriyaki Sauce (recipe follows)
    Water chestnut slices or green onion (white
        part only)

Cut meats into bite-sized pieces and pour over the Teriyaki Sauce. Marinate, covered, in the refrigerator for 1 hour. Remove from sauce. (Cover and chill if made ahead.)

Just before serving, place on a broiler pan about 4 inches from the heat until meat is no longer pink inside (about 5 minutes). Serve with water chestnut slices or green onion to be eaten with the meat. Offer picks to spear the meat and vegetables. Makes about 70 appetizers.

*Teriyaki Sauce.* Combine ⅓ cup soy sauce, 2 tablespoons sugar and sherry, ¾ teaspoon grated fresh ginger (or ¼ teaspoon ground ginger), and 2 cloves garlic (minced or mashed).

## Ginger-Minted Baby Carrots

Calorie counters may enjoy these tempting appetizers. Prepare and refrigerate them a day ahead if you like.

3 packages (10 oz. each) frozen baby carrots
1 cup orange juice
1 teaspoon grated fresh ginger
    Dash each salt and pepper
1 tablespoon chopped fresh mint

Combine carrots, orange juice, ginger, salt, and pepper in a pan. Cover and bring to boil; simmer until the carrots are just tender (about 3 minutes). Chill carrots, covered in liquid. Drain and spoon into serving bowl; garnish carrots with the fresh chopped mint. Serve with picks to guests. Makes about 6 cups.

## Melon Appetizer

Pile melon balls in a crystal bowl with a few lime slices to make a colorful appetizer fruit cocktail. Garnish with a few mint sprigs, if you like.

1 each medium-sized Crenshaw melon and
    medium-sized Persian melon
2 tablespoons lime juice
2 tablespoons honey
¼ teaspoon each ground coriander and nutmeg

Cut melons in halves, remove seeds. Cut fruit into balls of varying sizes, using melon ball cutter or metal measuring spoon. Place fruit and all juices in a deep bowl. Blend lime juice, honey, coriander, and nutmeg with the melon. Cover and chill. Spoon into serving bowls. Makes 8 to 10 servings.

## Meatballs Oregano

These meatballs will serve a crowd. They can all bake at the same time in the oven, and you can make them in advance.

*6 slices white bread*
*1 cup milk*
*1 cup finely chopped onion*
*2 tablespoons butter or margarine*
*4 pounds lean ground beef*
*¾ cup finely chopped parsley*
*4 egg yolks*
*4 teaspoons salt*
*¼ teaspoon pepper*
*¾ cup red wine vinegar*
*1 teaspoon oregano leaves*

Crumble the bread and soak in a bowl with the milk for 5 minutes; beat with a fork until mushy. Sauté the onion in the butter until golden. In a large mixing bowl, place the ground beef, parsley, egg yolks, milk mixture, sautéed onions, salt, and pepper. Thoroughly mix with your hands. Shape into 1¼-inch balls and place on two 10 by 15-inch baking pans. Bake in a 450° oven for 15 minutes or until meatballs are browned and slightly pink in the center.

Meanwhile, bring the vinegar and oregano to a boil over medium heat and let simmer 10 minutes; pour half the mixture over the hot meatballs in each pan, scraping up the pan juices. Serve immediately or leave in pan and chill, covered, or freeze. To serve at a later time, thaw, if frozen, and heat in the oven at 375° for 15 minutes. Serve warm with wooden picks. Makes about 6 dozen.

## Crunchy Toasted Indian Snack

A spicy snack from India contains a mixture of crunchy surprises—dried lentils, split peas, rice, nuts, and sesame seeds. Raisins add a soft, contrasting texture and sweetness.

*¼ cup each uncooked lentils, regular long grain rice, and split peas*
*About 3 cups water*
*2 tablespoons salad oil*
*1 tablespoon sesame seed*
*1 teaspoon each ground coriander and ground cumin*
*½ teaspoon ground turmeric*
*½ cup each roasted salted peanuts and cashews*
*¼ cup raisins*
*⅛ to ¼ teaspoon cayenne*
*¼ teaspoon ground cloves*
*1 teaspoon salt*
*Tortilla chips or potato chips (optional)*

Rinse the lentils, rice, and peas, and place in a pan with the 3 cups water; bring to a boil and boil 1 minute. Remove from heat, cover, and set aside for 10 minutes. Drain and rinse with cold water; spread on paper towels and pat dry.

In a wide frying pan, heat the oil over medium heat. Add the lentils, rice, peas, sesame seed, coriander, cumin, and turmeric. Cook, stirring until toasted (10 to 15 minutes). Remove from heat and stir in nuts, raisins, cayenne, cloves, and salt. Store airtight up to a week. To serve, pour into a bowl and surround with the chips for scooping or serve it plain as finger food. Makes 2 cups.

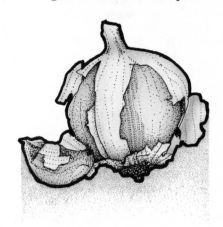

## Snails with Herb Butter

Canned snails are sold without shells, but you can purchase a container of snails plus reusable natural shells. These can be assembled early in the day.

*1 can of 18 (about 4 oz. drained weight) extra large cooked snails*
*½ cup (¼ lb.) soft butter*
*2 small cloves garlic, minced or mashed*
*2 teaspoons fresh, frozen, or freeze-dried chopped chives*
*1 tablespoon minced parsley*
*18 clean, dry snail shells, real or artificial*
*6 to 8 tablespoons grated Parmesan cheese French bread or rolls*

Drain snails, rinse, then spread on paper towels to drain. Mix butter with garlic, chives, and parsley until evenly blended. Put a small bit of butter in each shell, then tuck in a snail. Seal in with remaining butter. Press buttered surface firmly into the grated cheese. Arrange shells, cheese side up, in 3 snail pans (6-snail size) or 3 individual baking pans. Cover and chill until ready to cook. Bake, uncovered, in a 500° oven for 7 minutes or until cheese is lightly browned and butter is bubbling. Serve with bread to soak up the butter. Makes 3 first course servings of 6 snails each.

# Easy-to-Make Fresh Garlic Herb Cheese

All you need is milk or cream, buttermilk, a few seasonings, and a few minutes each day a few days in a row. The results compare remarkably in taste and texture to the delicate French boursin cheese.

Start with skim or whole milk, light (half-and-half) or heavy cream (whipping cream). Skim milk makes a tart but surprisingly rich tasting cheese; cream makes velvety, cool tasting cheese; whole milk and light cream produce subtle variations within this range. Also the yield of cheese from cream is more than double that of milk.

Heat 2 quarts of skim or whole milk (if using milk) or 1 quart light cream or 3 cups heavy cream (if using cream). Heat until lukewarm (90° to 100°) and pour into a bowl. Stir 4 tablespoons buttermilk into the skim or whole milk or stir only 2 tablespoons buttermilk into the light or heavy cream. Peel 8 cloves garlic and tie them loosely in a well washed cheesecloth, then crush lightly with the back of a spoon. Add the bag of garlic to the warm liquid and let stand at room temperature for 24 to 48 hours until a soft curd is formed (it should look like very soft yogurt and should not flow like a liquid when the bowl is slightly tilted). The curd forms faster on hot days than on cool ones.

Line a colander with a muslin cloth and set in the sink; pour the curd into the cloth and lift out the garlic bag squeezing it with your hand to force as much of the juice as possible into the curd. Drain the curd for about 10 minutes.

Fold cloth over the top of the curd to cover it. Position a wire rack on a pan (of somewhat larger dimensions than the colander) so that there is at least 1 inch between rack and pan bottom. Set colander on rack and cover the whole unit with clear plastic film to make airtight. Place this package in the refrigerator and let the curd drain 12 to 18 hours.

Spoon the drained curd from the cloth into a clean bowl and stir in ¾ teaspoon salt, ½ teaspoon basil leaves, and ¼ teaspoon each tarragon leaves, thyme leaves, rosemary leaves, and rubbed sage. Discard whey accumulated beneath colander.

For cheese molds use small natural finished baskets (not varnished, dyed, or painted) and rinse well with cool water, or use ceramic *coeur à la crème* molds. Molds of 1 cup or smaller capacity produce cheese of optimum firmness; if you use slightly larger molds, fill with no more than 1 cup curd. Line molds with 4 layers of well-washed cheesecloth, letting cloth drape over sides of the mold.

Spoon the curd into molds, and loosely fold cloth ends over the top. Set molds on the rack over the pan, the same one you used for draining the curd (washed) and tightly wrap clear plastic film over all. Return to the refrigerator and let drain overnight or for no longer than 48 hours.

To serve, pull cloth back from cheese and turn out onto a plate. Or you can wrap the unmolded cheese air tight and store in the refrigerator for as long as 5 days. Makes about 2 cups.

# Soups

*Savory and Satisfying*

## HELPFUL HINTS

Spice up canned condensed split pea soup by melting 1 tablespoon butter with 1 teaspoon each curry powder and instant minced onion. Combine with a 10-ounce can of the soup that has been diluted according to label directions. Heat and serve.

Add flavor to canned condensed tomato soup by mixing a 10-ounce can of the soup with ½ soup can water, ¼ teaspoon basil leaves, and 3 tablespoons Sherry. Heat thoroughly and serve sprinkled with shredded Parmesan cheese.

To make a quick, hot vegetable broth, combine a 24-ounce can of cocktail vegetable juice with 2 or 3 teaspoons beef stock base; heat thoroughly. Serve topped with fresh or freeze-dried chives.

For rich, flavorful soup, cook 1 cup sliced (about 4) carrots in 2 cups regular strength chicken broth until tender. Place all in a blender and add ½ teaspoon summer savory; whirl until smooth. Return to saucepan, stir in 2 tablespoons evaporated milk or whipping cream, reheat, and serve garnished with lime or lemon slice.

Make a cool soup to sip before dinner by blending 2 parts chilled canned chile-seasoned tomato cocktail or Bloody Mary mix with 1 part chilled canned clam juice. Add a squeeze of lime or lemon juice. Serve in mugs or glasses.

For a first course, chill canned madrilene or consommé (found in specialty food stores) for about 4 hours until set, then turn out and break up with a fork. Top each portion with a dollop of sour cream, finely minced chives, and freshly ground pepper.

## Mushroom Soup Paprika

Fresh mushroom soup gets a wonderful tang from the sour cream you blend with the broth just before serving. You can prepare the soup ahead of time and reheat for the final steps.

½ pound fresh mushrooms
1 tablespoon butter or margarine
1 teaspoon paprika
1 tablespoon all-purpose flour
2 tablespoons finely chopped parsley
4 cups regular strength beef broth (or beef concentrate dissolved in 4 cups hot water)
1 egg yolk
½ pint (1 cup) sour cream

Wash and slice mushrooms thinly into a saucepan. Sauté in butter along with paprika for 5 minutes or until golden brown. Sprinkle mushrooms with flour and parsley. Gradually stir in beef broth and simmer slowly for 30 minutes. Beat egg yolk slightly, then blend with sour cream and turn into a soup tureen. Pour the hot soup over it gradually, stirring well. Ladle into soup bowls. Makes 6 servings.

## Indian-Style Split Pea Soup

Serve this spicy split pea soup for a lunch or as an opening course. It has traditional curry seasonings.

1 ham hock (about 1 lb.), cracked
   Water
1½ cups green or yellow split peas
1 small onion, chopped
1 teaspoon each ground coriander and ground cumin
¼ teaspoon ground turmeric
1 teaspoon lemon juice
4 teaspoons sugar
   Salt and pepper
2 tablespoons chopped fresh coriander or parsley
   Chopped salted peanuts

Place ham hock in a Dutch oven, cover with water, cover pan, and bring to a boil. Simmer 10 minutes; drain.

Rinse and pick over split peas; add to the ham hock with 1½ quarts water and onion. Cover and simmer for about 1½ hours or until peas mash readily. Remove ham hock; discard bone and fat; cut meat into small pieces and return to pan. Add the ground coriander, cumin, turmeric, lemon juice, sugar, salt, and pepper to taste. Simmer 10

minutes longer. Serve with fresh coriander and chopped peanuts. Makes about 6 servings.

## Spanish Garlic Soup

Sopa de Ajo consists of hot chicken broth, buttery toast, and eggs—a delightful first course to any meal.

4 slices firm white bread
2 tablespoons butter or margarine
3 cloves garlic, minced or mashed
2 cans (14 oz. each) regular strength chicken broth
1 bay leaf
1 teaspoon lemon juice
4 eggs
   Finely chopped parsley or coarsely chopped fresh coriander

Trim crusts from bread; cut bread into ½-inch cubes. In a large frying pan, melt butter; add garlic and bread cubes and cook over medium heat, stirring often, until bread is lightly browned. Remove from pan; reserve. In the pan, combine broth, bay leaf, and lemon juice; bring to a simmer. Break eggs, one at a time, into a saucer; carefully slip each into the hot broth. Poach eggs for 4 minutes or until whites are set and yolks are still runny. Spoon eggs into 4 soup bowls; ladle broth over top and sprinkle with croutons and parsley. Makes 4 servings.

## Chile with Coriander

Mexicans serve bowls of hot chile con carne topped with avocado slices and lots of freshly chopped coriander leaves.

1 teaspoon salt
1 pound lean ground beef
1 medium-sized onion, chopped
1 can (14 oz.) pear shaped tomatoes
1 large can (1 lb. 11 oz.) red kidney beans
1½ teaspoons chile powder
1 teaspoon oregano
½ teaspoon ground cumin
   Sliced avocado
¼ cup coarsely chopped fresh coriander

(Continued on next page)

Sprinkle salt into a 10-inch frying pan; add ground beef and onion, stirring until browned (about 5 minutes), then add tomatoes, kidney beans, chile powder, oregano, and cumin. Simmer, uncovered, stirring occasionally for about 15 minutes. Garnish each serving with several slices of avocado and pass a dish of coarsely chopped coriander. Makes about 4 servings.

## Lentils and Ham Soup

A hearty supper soup of rich ham hocks, lentils, vegetables, and pitted dried prunes creates some interesting sweet, spicy flavors.

    3½ to 4 pounds ham hocks, cut in 2-inch slices
        Water
    2 bay leaves
    1 teaspoon Italian herb seasoning or oregano
        leaves
    1 teaspoon whole mixed pickling spices
    ⅛ teaspoon pepper
    1 medium-sized onion, chopped
    1½ cups lentils
    6 small new potatoes, peeled, or 2 cups carrot
        chunks
    12 to 16 pitted whole prunes
        Chopped parsley

Put the ham hocks into a large pot, cover with water, bring to boiling, then drain and discard liquid. Return ham to pot, add 12 cups water, bay leaf, Italian herbs, pickling spice, pepper, and onion. Simmer for about 2 hours or until ham begins to come away from bones. Pour through wire strainer and discard seasonings. When cool enough to handle, return meat and broth to the cooking pot; discard skin and bones. Skim excess fat from broth, bring to boiling again, and add lentils. Cover and simmer about 20 minutes, add potatoes (or carrots) and prunes, and simmer about 25 minutes or until tender. Garnish with parsley. Makes 6 to 8 servings.

## Golden Carrot Soup with Mint

Whirl the cooked carrots in a blender to a fine purée. Then finish off the soup with broiled cream topping.

    2 cups peeled, sliced carrots (about 4 carrots)
    1 cup boiling water
    ½ teaspoon salt
    2 tablespoons chopped onion
    1½ teaspoons chopped fresh or dried mint
    2 tablespoons melted butter or margarine
    2 tablespoons all-purpose flour
    2 cups regular strength chicken broth or milk
    ¼ teaspoon ground nutmeg
        Salt to taste
    ¾ cup orange juice
    ½ cup whipping cream
    ¼ teaspoon grated orange peel
        Dash ground nutmeg

In a saucepan, cook carrots in water and salt until tender. Whirl carrots and cooking liquid smooth in a blender. In another saucepan, sauté onion and mint in butter until soft. Mix in flour and stir until bubbly; gradually add chicken broth or milk, the carrot mixture, and the ¼ teaspoon nutmeg. Simmer over medium-low heat, stirring, for 3 to 4 minutes. Add salt to taste and stir in orange juice.

Pour into heat-proof soup bowls. Lightly whip cream; add grated orange peel and a dash of nutmeg. Spoon even portions of cream onto each bowl of soup; set under broiler until top is nicely browned. Makes 4 servings.

## Chilled Cucumber Bisque

Basil-enhanced cucumber bisque is served chilled. Sour cream is beaten in just at the last minute.

    3 large or 4 medium-sized cucumbers
    2 cups regular strength chicken broth
    ½ teaspoon salt
    ⅛ teaspoon pepper
    2 tablespoons coarsely chopped fresh basil or
        1 teaspoon dried basil leaves
    ¼ cup (⅛ lb.) butter or margarine
    ½ cup sour cream

Peel and slice cucumbers into ¼-inch pieces (you should have about 2 quarts). Put cucumber pieces in a saucepan with chicken broth, salt, pepper, basil, and butter; simmer, covered, for 5 minutes (stirring once midway) or until cucumbers are tender when pierced with a fork.

Pour broth and cucumbers into blender container (half at a time); whirl until smooth. Pour through wire strainer into large bowl, mashing with a spoon. Repeat with remaining cucumbers and broth. Cover and refrigerate 3 hours or more.

Just before serving, beat in sour cream with rotary beater. Makes 4 to 6 servings.

## Condiment Soup

Ideal for dieters and non-dieters alike, this soup makes a cool, refreshing focal point for a luncheon or dinner. Dill, parsley, and mint combine with yogurt and chicken broth. Offer condiments of a chopped cucumber, thinly sliced green onion, chopped hard-cooked egg, sweet raisins, and salted cashews.

1 quart (4 cups) unflavored yogurt
1 can (about 14 oz.) regular strength chicken broth
½ cup cold water
1 tablespoon minced parsley
1 teaspoon each dill weed and minced fresh or crushed dried mint
Salt to taste
Dash cayenne
½ cup each golden raisins, thinly sliced green onions (including some tops), and chopped salted cashews
2 hard-cooked eggs, finely chopped
1 cucumber, peeled and chopped

Smoothly blend yogurt, broth, and water. Then add parsley, dill weed, mint, salt, and cayenne; chill, covered. Present the soup in a tureen or in individual bowls. Have raisins, onions, cashews, eggs, and cucumber in separate dishes and pass for diners to add, according to individual tastes. Makes 6 servings.

## Vegetable Soup with Herb Butter Balls

Fresh garden herbs are blended with butter and shaped into balls, seasoning this hot soup as they melt.

½ pound asparagus
1 medium-sized carrot
2 small new potatoes
5 cups regular strength chicken or beef broth
1 tablespoon lemon juice
⅓ cup thinly sliced green onions
Herb Butter Balls (directions follow)

Cut tough ends from asparagus and discard; cut spears diagonally into ½-inch slanting slices.

Scrape or peel the carrot and dice into pieces about ⅓-inch square. Peel potatoes and cut into ½-inch cubes.

In a saucepan, combine chicken broth and lemon juice and bring to boiling. Add the potatoes, cover; when boiling resumes, cook 5 minutes. Add the carrots, cover, and cook 5 minutes more. Add the asparagus and green onions, cook 5 minutes or until vegetables are just tender. Ladle soup into bowls and serve Herb Butter Balls so diners can season soups individually. Makes 6 to 8 servings.

Herb Butter Balls. In a small bowl, mix together until blended 4 tablespoons (⅛ lb.) slightly softened butter or margarine and 2 teaspoons minced parsley. Then add one of these fresh herbs: 1 teaspoon minced tarragon leaves, basil leaves, or rosemary leaves, or 2 teaspoons chopped chives. If you don't have fresh herbs, use ½ teaspoon of one of the dried herbs or 2 teaspoons frozen or freeze-dried chives. Shape mixture into a ball and float in ice water until firm. Cut ball into 16 equal portions. Using chilled wooden butter paddles or your hands, shape portions into balls. Chill balls in ice water. Serve on ice.

## Fish and Potato Selyanka

Selyanka is a Finnish name given to a number of dishes combining meat or fish with vegetables. Made with halibut, this soup is country-style and fragrant with dill.

2 pounds halibut steaks or Greenland turbot fillets
6 cups regular strength chicken broth
1 pound new potatoes, peeled and cut in ½-inch cubes
1 large onion, finely chopped
1 teaspoon dill weed
1 medium-sized white or red onion (mild flavor, if available), chopped
6 tablespoons melted butter
Salt and pepper
Dill weed

(Continued on next page)

Place fish in a saucepan and add broth. Cover and bring to a boil over medium heat; then reduce heat and simmer 2 to 4 minutes or until fish breaks easily when prodded. Set aside for at least 20 minutes (or you can chill fish in broth to intensify the fish flavor); then lift out fish with a slotted or runcible spoon. Remove and discard any skin and bones; cut fish in bite-sized chunks.

Return saucepan with broth to high heat. Add potatoes, the large chopped onion, and the 1 teaspoon dill weed. Boil, covered, for about 10 minutes or until potatoes are tender enough to mash. Add fish and heat through.

Ladle soup into bowls; add to individual servings the chopped uncooked onion, melted butter, salt, and pepper to taste; add an additional sprinkling of dill weed. Makes 5 to 6 main dish or 8 to 10 first course servings.

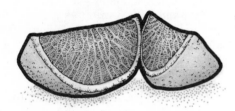

## Shrimp Bisque

What makes these soups thick and creamy is cooking the vegetables with the shellfish and then blending them all into a purée. You'd be surprised how few calories are in each serving.

*½ pound raw shrimp in shells*
*3 cups water*
*1 medium-sized onion*
*4 sprigs parsley*
*1 whole clove*
*2 tablespoons butter*
*1 small carrot, sliced*
*1 teaspoon paprika*
*2 tablespoons uncooked rice*
*¼ cup dry white wine*
*2 tablespoons milk or half-and-half (light cream)*
*4 teaspoons lemon juice*
*About ¼ teaspoon liquid hot pepper seasoning*
*Salt and pepper to taste*

Shell and devein the shrimp, saving all the shells; set aside shrimp. Put shells in a pan with the water, half of the onion (sliced), parsley, and clove. Bring to boiling, then cover and simmer for 30 minutes. Strain broth, pressing out all liquid, then discard the shells and vegetables. Measure broth and, if necessary, add water to make 3 cups liquid.

In a Dutch oven or other heavy pan, melt the butter, add remaining onion (chopped), the carrot, and paprika; sauté slowly until these vegetables are very soft (about 10 minutes). Stir in the strained broth, rice, and wine. Cover and simmer until rice is soft (about 30 minutes). Add shrimp and cook until they turn pink (about 3 to 5 minutes). Set aside 6 of the shrimp, then whirl rest of soup mixture, a part at a time, in a blender until smooth. Return to the pan; add the milk, lemon juice, hot pepper seasoning, and salt and pepper to taste.

When ready to serve, reheat slowly and stir in reserved shrimp, chopped. Makes about 1 quart soup.

## Goulash Soup

If you have time, it's best to make this soup a day or two ahead. Refrigerate, skim, then reheat it.

*3 pounds boneless beef chuck, cubed*
*2 tablespoons each salad oil and butter or margarine*
*2 large onions, chopped*
*1 small clove garlic, minced or mashed*
*1 tablespoon sweet Hungarian paprika or regular paprika*
*5 cups water*
*1 large green pepper, seeded and cut in strips*
*2 teaspoons salt*
*⅛ teaspoon pepper*
*1 teaspoon caraway seed*
*2 tomatoes, peeled, seeded, and coarsely chopped*
*1 small, dried, hot chile pepper, crushed (optional)*
*2 medium-sized potatoes, cut in eighths*

Brown meat, about one quarter at a time, in heated oil in a large deep pan (at least a 4-qt. size); remove and reserve meat. When all is browned, pour off any pan drippings and discard them; melt butter in the same pan over medium heat. Add onions and garlic and cook until onions are soft and golden (do not brown); blend in paprika. Stir in meat and juices, water, green pepper, salt, pepper, caraway seed, chopped tomatoes, and chile (if used).

Bring soup to a boil, reduce heat, cover, and simmer for about 2 hours or until meat is almost tender. If possible at this point, cool the soup slightly, cover, and refrigerate for several hours or overnight; skim off fat, then bring soup to a simmer again. Add potatoes and cook for 20 to 30 minutes more or until both potatoes and meat are tender. Serve soup steaming hot. Makes 6 servings.

# Growing Herbs in the Kitchen

A window box or hanging basket of growing herbs in the kitchen can be a pleasurable, aromatic addition to the room. Whatever container you decide on or herbs you select, the effect can be very gratifying for the cook.

## Which Herbs to Choose

Many nurseries offer a wide selection of herbs in small pots that are already growing. These can be left in individual pots or transplanted to a flower box. Trailing herbs such as rosemary and thyme are very attractive in hanging pots, but even non-trailing kinds—basil, marjoram, mint, oregano, and sage—will spill over the container's edge as their stems grow longer. Other plants that are adaptable to inside gardens are chives, parsley, coriander, and chervil. You can grow parsley, chervil, coriander, sweet basil, and summer savory from seed.

## Planting Techniques

Use a clean, porous potting mixture and no fertilizer. If you mix your own, use equal parts of top soil, sand, and ground bark, leaf mold, or peat moss. Thin seedlings to several inches apart when 1 to 2 inches high. (Plant seeds directly in the ground outside if you don't want to grow them in the kitchen.)

## Necessary Growing Conditions

The inevitable trouble with many kitchens is their hot, dry atmosphere. Humidity should be between 30 to 50 percent. If it is less, place a bowl of water near the plants. As it evaporates, it moistens the air around each plant. Full sun is best for most herbs; exceptions adapted to partial shading include mint, parsley, chives, and chervil. Be careful that the reflected sunlight near a window is not so bright that it is burning the foliage. The temperature should be about 70° and the room should have fresh moving air (not a draft) for the best growing conditions.

Most herbs need only moderate watering after they are established. Mint, however, needs lots of water. All appreciate having their foliage frequently sprinkled or sprayed with water to freshen them up.

# Salads

## A Little Mint, Chile, or Dill Can Wake Up a Salad

### HELPFUL HINTS

Sauerkraut and apples combine for an easy salad. Drain a 1 pound can sauerkraut well and mix it with 1 tablespoon minced parsley, ½ teaspoon caraway seed, ⅛ teaspoon anise seed, 1 teaspoon sugar, and 2 tablespoons sour cream. Cover, chill, then add 1 medium-sized red apple, unpeeled and diced, and serve on lettuce leaves.

Sprinkle toasted sesame seeds generously over a crisp green salad for crunchiness.

One quick salad combines 1 cup chopped onion and 5 cups peeled, diced tomatoes with ⅓ cup minced fresh mint leaves. Cover and refrigerate for 2 hours. Season with salt and pepper.

A delicious, simple salad can be served in halved avocados on butter lettuce leaves. Fill with oil and vinegar dressing seasoned with chile powder to taste.

For a delightful new taste treat, let peeled papaya, cut in halves, marinate several hours in a tangy dressing of ¼ cup *each* salad oil and lemon juice, 1 tablespoon finely minced green onion, ½ teaspoon *each* chile powder and salt, and ¼ teaspoon pepper.

Spinach greens are enhanced by a pine nut dressing made by combining ½ cup chopped pine nuts with ¼ cup salad oil or olive oil, 3 tablespoons tarragon vinegar, ¼ teaspoon grated lemon peel, ½ teaspoon salt, and dash nutmeg. Toss with 1½ quarts spinach greens.

## Mushroom and Watercress Salad

Small scallop shells make attractive serving plates for this marinated salad.

    1 pound medium-sized mushrooms
    2 tablespoons each lemon juice and white wine
        vinegar
    ½ cup olive oil
    ½ teaspoon each salt and tarragon leaves,
        crumbled
    1 cup watercress leaves or chopped curly endive

Wash and slice the mushrooms; turn into a bowl. Mix together the lemon juice and vinegar, olive oil, salt, and tarragon. Pour dressing over mushrooms and let stand 1 hour or overnight, turning occasionally. Just before serving, add the watercress or endive and mix. Makes 6 to 8 servings.


## Oriental Chicken Salad

Arrange the chicken and vegetables on a large serving tray and prepare the dressing early in the day. Let each person assemble his own salad.

    Sesame Seed Dressing (recipe follows)
    2 to 3 whole chicken breasts (about 2 to 3 lbs.)
    Salted water
    Lettuce leaves
    6 to 8 ounces fresh bean sprouts
    1 can (5 or 6 oz.) water chestnuts
    2 ripe avocados, peeled, seeded, and thinly sliced
    2 or 3 peaches, peeled and sliced
    ⅔ cup toasted whole blanched almonds
    Lemon juice

Prepare Sesame Seed Dressing. Cover and chill several hours to blend flavors. Simmer chicken in a small amount of salted water until just tender when pierced (15 to 20 minutes). When cool enough to handle, discard skin and bones and break meat into large chunks. Arrange the chicken on a large lettuce-lined serving tray. Rinse the bean sprouts and drain well (or blanch sprouts for 1 minute in boiling water, rinse in cold water, and drain). Drain the water chestnuts and slice. Arrange bean sprouts and water chestnuts on tray with chicken. (This much can be done ahead; chill.)

Just before serving add the avocado slices, peach slices, and toasted almonds. (Dip avocado and peach slices in lemon juice to prevent discoloration.) Everyone assembles a salad. Makes 4 to 6 servings.

*Sesame Seed Dressing.* In a small bowl, combine ¼ cup olive oil, 1 tablespoon *each* lemon juice and

honey, 2 tablespoons toasted sesame seed, 1 teaspoon curry powder, 1 cup sour cream, salt, and pepper to taste. Cover and chill several hours to blend flavors.

## Tomato and Avocado Salad, Mogul Dressing

Chinese five-spice is the major flavoring in this dressing. It is a spice blend available in Oriental markets and many supermarkets.

    Mogul Dressing (recipe follows)
    2 large or 4 medium-sized tomatoes, peeled and
        thinly sliced
    2 avocados, peeled and sliced
    Cucumber slices and romaine leaves (optional)

Prepare the dressing 2 hours or longer before serving; set aside. Just before serving, arrange the tomato and avocado slices on a serving plate. Generously drizzle the prepared dressing over top, using about half of it. Serve additional dressing at the table. Garnish plate with the cucumber and romaine, if you wish. Makes 4 to 6 servings.

*Mogul Dressing.* Combine ½ cup salad oil, 2 tablespoons tarragon wine vinegar, 1 teaspoon *each* basil leaves and Chinese five-spice, ½ teaspoon *each* salt and lemon juice, 1 small clove garlic, minced or mashed, and ⅛ teaspoon *each* dry mustard and pepper. Beat with a fork to blend; let stand, then beat again just before serving.


## Sliced Tomatoes with Herb Dressing

First allow the herb flavors to mingle with each other, then pour over tomato slices.

    Basil or Tarragon Dressing (recipes, page 32)
    2 or 3 large or 6 medium-sized tomatoes
    Mild, sweet onion slices (optional)
    Freshly ground pepper to taste

*(Continued on next page)*

Prepare either of the herb dressings and set aside for 1 to 2 hours to mellow flavors. Peel the tomatoes or not, as you prefer, and slice them about $\frac{1}{4}$ inch thick. Overlap slices in a shallow bowl, tuck a few thin slices sweet onion between tomato slices, if you wish. Mix the dressing again and drizzle over tomatoes; serve or refrigerate for up to 1 hour. (If refrigerated, spoon dressing from bottom of bowl over tomatoes before serving.) Grind pepper over top. Makes 4 to 6 servings.

*Basil Dressing.* Combine in a blender container $\frac{1}{4}$ cup olive oil or salad oil (or half of each), 2 tablespoons garlic (or regular) red wine vinegar, $\frac{1}{2}$ teaspoon *each* salt and sugar, and $\frac{1}{4}$ cup fresh basil leaves (loosely packed in cup) or 1 tablespoon dried whole basil leaves; whirl until blended. (Without a blender, finely mince fresh basil or crush dried, then mix with other ingredients.)

*Tarragon Dressing.* Prepare the same as for Basil Dressing above, omitting the basil leaves. Add 1 teaspoon dried tarragon leaves and 2 teaspoons fresh or freeze-dried chives. Whirl in blender mix until blended.

## Dilled Potato Salad Tray

Combine a hearty salad with cold cuts and achieve a completely made-ahead menu to be served on a tray indoors or out.

1½ quarts cubed cooked potatoes (about 6 large
  potatoes)
¾ cup each unflavored yogurt and sour cream
1 teaspoon each dill weed, sugar, prepared
  mustard, celery seed, and salt
1½ cups sliced celery
1 cup each chopped green onions and sliced
  radishes
½ cup chopped parsley
6 hard-cooked eggs, shelled
  About 2 pounds cold sliced meat
  Pickles and olives

Put the potatoes in a large bowl. In a small bowl mix well the yogurt, sour cream, dill weed, sugar, mustard, celery seed, and salt; pour over the potatoes. Stir gently to coat the potatoes with dressing. Cover and refrigerate until chilled, several hours or overnight.

Shortly before serving, add the celery, green onions, radishes, and parsley to the potatoes. Dice 4 of the eggs and add to the salad, mixing carefully.

Mound the salad in the center of a large serving tray. Slice the 2 remaining eggs and arrange with meat, pickles, and olives around salad. Makes about 12 servings.

## Brown Rice Salad

Dates, cinnamon, and fresh orange slices lend a pleasant subtlety to brown rice salad.

2½ cups water
1½ cups quick-cooking brown rice
7 tablespoons lemon juice
½ cup olive oil or salad oil
¼ teaspoon ground cinnamon
½ cup each minced fresh parsley and mint
  (or ½ cup dried mint, crumbled)
¼ cup minced green onion, including some of
  the tops (optional)
  About ⅔ cup pitted dates
  About ½ teaspoon salt
3 large oranges
  Mint leaves or parsley sprigs

Bring water to boiling, add rice, cover, and cook on low heat for about 15 minutes or until rice is tender and liquid is absorbed. Pour rice into a bowl (it can be hot or cold) and add lemon juice, olive oil, cinnamon, parsley, mint, and onions. Finely chop $\frac{1}{3}$ cup of the dates and stir into the rice salad; add salt to taste. If the salad is warm, or if made ahead, cover and chill.

Mound rice into a shallow serving dish. Cut peel from oranges with a knife, then cut oranges in crosswise slices and decorate rice salad with the fruit slices, the remaining dates, and mint leaves. Makes 4 to 6 servings.

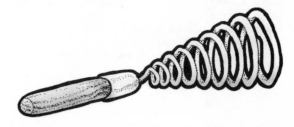

## Fresh Bean Salad

Cook and marinate the green beans in advance. Serve topped with onion rings.

1½ to 2 pounds fresh green beans or 3 packages
  (9 oz. each) frozen cut green beans
  Boiling salted water
½ cup salad oil
¼ cup tomato-based chile sauce
½ teaspoon dry mustard
½ teaspoon savory or rosemary leaves
¼ teaspoon salt
⅛ teaspoon pepper
1 clove garlic, minced or mashed
  Lettuce leaves
½ medium-sized onion
¼ cup wine vinegar

Cook the beans in the boiling water until just tender-crisp. Drain immediately, then rinse in cold water, drain again, and put into a bowl. Combine in a blender jar (or another jar) the oil, chile sauce, mustard, savory, salt, pepper, and garlic. Whirl or shake until blended. Pour dressing over the beans. Cover and refrigerate at least 4 hours or overnight.

At serving time, lift beans from marinade with a slotted spoon and arrange with lettuce in serving dish. Cut the onion in very thin slices, separate into rings, and distribute over beans. Blend the vinegar into remaining marinade, drizzle some over beans, and serve the rest at the table. Makes about 6 servings.

## Mediterranean Eggplant Salad

Eggplant combines with brown rice in this typical Mediterranean-style salad. It's served cool and can be assembled up to two hours before serving.

    2 teaspoons olive oil or salad oil
    ½ cup long grain brown rice
    1¼ cups water
    ½ teaspoon salt
    1 eggplant (about 1¼ lbs.)
    2 tablespoons olive or salad oil
      Water
    ¾ teaspoon each salt and ground cumin
    1 teaspoon ground cinnamon
    ¼ cup finely chopped mint
    1 cup thinly sliced celery
    ½ cup sliced green onion with some of the tops
      Lemon Dressing (recipe follows)
      Lettuce leaves
      2 large tomatoes cut in wedges
      Unflavored yogurt

Heat the 2 teaspoons oil in a small saucepan over high heat. Stir in the brown rice until coated. Add the 1¼ cups water and ½ teaspoon salt; cover and simmer for about 45 minutes or until rice is just tender and liquid is absorbed. Remove from heat and set aside.

Meanwhile, wash the eggplant and trim away stem. Cut into ¾-inch cubes. Heat the 2 tablespoons oil in a 10-inch frying pan (one with a tight fitting lid) over medium-high heat; add eggplant and cook, stirring, until eggplant starts to brown (3 to 5 minutes). Add 2 tablespoons water, cover pan, and reduce heat to medium. Uncover pan at 1 to 2-minute intervals and stir, adding about 2 tablespoons water at a time as it is absorbed; stir as necessary until completely tender and all liquid absorbed (about 15 minutes total cooking time). Remove from heat and stir in the ¾ teaspoon salt,

cumin, and cinnamon. Turn into a large bowl, stir in rice, and cool to room temperature. Then mix in the mint, celery, green onion, and Lemon Dressing. Cover and chill for 1 to 2 hours.

To serve, heap the eggplant salad in a shallow bowl lined with lettuce leaves. Garnish with the tomato wedges. At the table pass a small bowl of the unflavored yogurt for extra seasoning. Makes about 6 servings.

*Lemon Dressing.* In a small bowl, mix 1 tablespoon olive oil or salad oil, 5 tablespoons lemon juice, 1 tablespoon sugar, ½ teaspoon salt, ¼ teaspoon liquid hot pepper seasoning, and 1 small clove garlic, minced or mashed.

## Mexican Cucumber and Orange Salad Tray

Strongly reminiscent of Mexico's *pico de gallo* relish, this salad features oranges, cucumbers, onions, avocado, and chile dressing.

    2 medium-sized cucumbers
    ⅓ cup white wine vinegar
    ½ cup olive oil or salad oil
    ½ teaspoon salt
    1 large mild onion (red or white), cut in thin
      vertical slices
    4 large oranges, peeled with a knife to remove
      white membrane, cut in crosswise slices
    1 large avocado, peeled and sliced
      About 1 tablespoon lemon juice
      Butter lettuce leaves
      Orange-Chile Dressing (recipe, page 34)

With a vegetable parer, peel lengthwise strips from each cucumber, making alternating patterns of green and white. Thinly slice cucumbers and place in a bowl, adding vinegar, oil, and salt. Mix, cover, and chill at least 1 hour.

On a large rimmed tray, arrange separately side by side the cucumbers (lift from marinade, saving marinade), onions, oranges, and avocado; drizzle lemon juice over avocado to preserve color. Garnish tray with lettuce. If made ahead, cover with clear plastic film and chill up to 5 hours. When serving, spoon the Orange-Chile Dressing onto individual portions. Makes 8 to 10 servings.

*Orange-Chile Dressing.* Add to reserved cucumber marinade 1½ teaspoons grated orange peel, ½ teaspoon chile powder, and ¼ teaspoon salt; do not refrigerate. Blend and pour into a small bowl.

## Green Salad with Sesame Seed Dressing

You can prepare the dressing the night or the morning before serving. Wash and chill the salad greens.

½ *cup sesame seed*
1 *cup sour cream*
2 *teaspoons sugar*
1 *teaspoon onion salt*
⅛ *teaspoon pepper*
1 *tablespoon vinegar*
1 *teaspoon Worcestershire*
1 *clove garlic, minced or mashed*
2½ *quarts torn greens*

Toast the sesame seed in a frying pan over medium-low heat, stirring frequently until browned. Remove from heat and let cool. Mix together the sour cream, sugar, onion salt, pepper, vinegar, Worcestershire, and garlic; stir in toasted seeds. Chill.

Just before serving, mix dressing with the greens and serve. Makes 6 servings.

## Summer Slaw

The light oil and vinegar dressing for this cabbage salad has a pleasantly sweet-tart flavor.

1 *medium-sized head cabbage (about 2 lbs.)*
2 *medium-sized mild white onions*
½ *cup each sugar and cider vinegar*
1 *teaspoon each dry mustard and salt*
⅛ *teaspoon pepper*
1 *teaspoon celery seed*
½ *cup salad oil*
 *Cherry tomato halves*

Finely shred the cabbage (you should have 8 cups). Thinly slice the onions and separate them into rings. In a large bowl alternate layers of the cabbage and onion rings.

In a saucepan, combine the sugar, vinegar, mustard, salt, pepper, and celery seed. Bring to a boil,

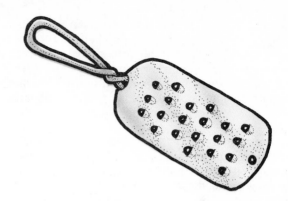

stirring until the sugar is dissolved. Remove from heat, mix in the salad oil, then pour dressing over the cabbage and onions. Allow the salad to cool slightly, then cover and refrigerate for at least 4 hours or overnight, stirring several times.

Use a slotted spoon to lift the cabbage and onions out of the dressing, then heap into a serving bowl. Garnish with cherry tomatoes. Makes 6 to 8 servings.

## Minted Tuna Salad

Fresh mint and limes give a refreshing flavor to this whole-meal salad.

½ *teaspoon grated lime peel*
3 *tablespoons lime juice*
2 *tablespoons chopped fresh mint*
2 *cans (about 6 oz. each) chunk style tuna, drained*
1½ *cups cold cooked rice*
1 *cup each thinly sliced celery and frozen peas, thawed*
2 *tablespoons each chopped green onion and parsley*
 *Tangy Dressing (recipe follows)*
 *Salt and pepper*
 *Crisp greens and mint sprigs*

Combine the lime peel and juice and mint leaves; set aside. In a bowl, combine the tuna, rice, celery, peas, green onion, and parsley. Pour over the lime-mint mixture, stir well, cover, and refrigerate for 2 to 4 hours. Prepare dressing, cover, and refrigerate.

To serve, pour the dressing below over the tuna mixture, and mix gently. Season to taste with salt and pepper. Turn into a lettuce-lined salad bowl and garnish with mint sprigs. Makes 6 servings.

*Tangy Dressing.* Combine 1 teaspoon Dijon mustard, 2 teaspoons sugar, and ½ teaspoon liquid hot pepper seasoning. Gradually add ½ cup mayonnaise and ¼ cup buttermilk. Stir until well blended.

# How to Make Herb Vinegars

Fresh garden herbs and whole spices are ideal ingredients for flavoring vinegars. Whether you grow your own herbs, buy them from your market, or get them in pots from the nursery, making vinegar is an extremely simple process. You need to allow several weeks for the vinegar to stand and infuse the herbs' flavors; the effect is softening and mellows the vinegar's sharp flavor, resulting in delightful blends.

## What herbs to use

In addition to the ones we give here, try fresh dill, varieties of thyme, parsley, garlic, shallots, or green onions.

## How to proceed

Put your choice of flavoring herb into a clean jar or decorative bottle. Fill it with cider or wine vinegar and put on the lid or cap. To speed up the infusion so you can start enjoying the vinegar in one or two weeks, heat it to lukewarm (or even boiling), then pour into bottles over bruised or coarsely chopped herb leaves. Let the bottles stand in a warm place (a sunny window sill) and shake gently each day. When the flavor suits you, strain out the seasonings and discard, then return the vinegar to the bottle.

To make clear vinegars that have the whole herbs intact, you must allow more time for the infusion process. Do not bruise the herb leaves or heat the vinegar at all, and let the bottles stand in a cool, dark place without shaking them. It takes about three to four weeks for the flavor to develop.

## Vinegar Recipes

**Lemon Thyme and Rosemary Vinegar.** Wash and dry 1 leafy sprig (about 5 inches long) *each* rosemary and lemon thyme. Place herbs in a pint bottle with 4 whole black peppers and 5 small fresh grapes; fill the bottle with white wine vinegar.

**Sweet Basil and Oregano Vinegar (or Tarragon Vinegar).** Wash and dry 1 leafy sprig (about 5 inches long) *each* sweet basil and oregano (or use 2 sprigs fresh tarragon). Place herbs in a pint bottle with 4 whole black peppers and fill with red wine vinegar.

**Lemon-Mint Vinegar.** With a small sharp knife, cut a continuous spiral strip of peel about ¼ inch wide from 1 lemon. Wash and dry 2 leafy sprigs of mint. Place mint, lemon rind, and 6 dried currants in a pint bottle and fill with white wine vinegar.

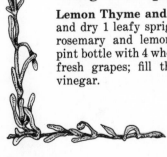

# Meats

*Seasoning Suggestions for Beef, Pork, and Lamb*

When barbecuing thick beef chuck or flank steak, spread each side generously with your favorite prepared mustard. Sprinkle with salt and cook until browned on each side and done as you like it.

Add a crunchy topping to steak by toasting 2 teaspoons sesame seed until richly browned in a dry frying pan. Combine with ¼ cup melted butter and 1 minced clove garlic. pour over 2 servings of broiled steak just before serving.

For a tender, succulent veal treat pound 1½ pounds thinly sliced veal cutlet to about ¼-inch thick. Cut into serving sized pieces and sauté both sides in 1 tablespoon butter. Add juice of 1 lemon, salt and pepper to taste, and 2 teaspoons minced fresh tarragon or 1 teaspoon dried tarragon leaves that were previously soaked in lemon juice. Cook over medium heat until tender.

About 1 hour before barbecuing beef or pork steaks rub surface with a cut clove of garlic. Then rub in Chinese five-spice, using about ½ teaspoon for 1½ pounds of meat. A new taste treat.

Make a super sandwich by barbecuing or broiling a flank steak, slicing it thin, and arranging it on hot bread slices, alternating meat strips with thin slices Meunster cheese. Sprinkle with ground cumin seed.

Sprinkle rosemary leaves over coals when barbecuing meat for a fresh herb flavor. Also tie branches of fresh rosemary together at one end and use as a basting brush when barbecuing meat, especially lamb.

A tasty accompaniment or garnish for a main meat dish is French fried parsley. You wash and dry it well, then drop sprigs into hot deep fat (370°) for about 3 seconds. Drain and salt generously.

## Pepper Steak (Steak au Poivre)

Grind a light coating of pepper over steaks and let chill before pan-cooking.

1½ to 2-pound sirloin or top round steak, cut
    ¾ inch thick
    About 2 teaspoons freshly ground pepper or
    cracked whole peppers
3 tablespoons butter or margarine
    Salt
2 tablespoons finely chopped onions or shallots
½ cup beef stock (use 1 teaspoon beef stock base
    plus ½ cup water)
2 to 4 tablespoons brandy, Cognac, or Madeira

If you wish, you can cut meat into serving-sized pieces and use unseasoned meat tenderizer as the package directs.

Grind pepper from a pepper mill over both sides of the meat to coat lightly (about 2 teaspoons) or press in cracked whole peppers. Chill at least 1 hour.

Melt 1 tablespoon of the butter in a large frying pan over high heat. Add meat and sauté quickly (about 4 minutes on a side or until well browned and still slightly pink inside). Season with salt to taste and remove from pan to a hot platter.

Melt another 1 tablespoon butter in pan, add the onions, and sauté until golden. Pour in stock and boil until reduced by half. Add 2 tablespoons of the brandy, Cognac, or Madeira, and bring back to boiling. Add remaining 1 tablespoon butter and stir until blended; then spoon over steak. If you wish, warm 2 tablespoons brandy in a metal cup, ignite, and spoon flaming over the meat at the table. Makes about 4 servings.

## Orange-Thyme Beef Roast

Juice squeezed from an orange adds freshness and an enriched meaty flavor rather than the fruity overtones you might expect.

4½ to 5-pound sirloin tip, top round, or cross
    rib roast
1½ teaspoons grated orange peel
½ teaspoon thyme leaves
⅓ cup each wine vinegar and salad oil
1 medium-sized orange, cut in half
    Salt

Place roast in a deep bowl or heavy plastic bag. Add orange peel, thyme, vinegar, and salad oil; rub over surfaces of meat. Cover and refrigerate 4 hours to overnight; turn meat occasionally. Lift meat from marinade, reserving liquid. Place meat on a rack in a pan and roast in a 325° oven for about 2 hours for rare meat. (A thermometer inserted in thickest part will register 135°.) Baste meat occasionally with marinade. Skim fat from pan and discard; squeeze in juice of the orange and accompany sliced beef with pan juices. Season with salt to taste. Makes 8 to 10 servings.

## Simmered Corned Beef

You cook this corned beef ahead so it can chill in the cooking liquid. It's great for a picnic take-along.

About 5 pounds corned beef, bottom round, or
   brisket
Water
1 medium-sized onion, chopped
¼ teaspoon each garlic powder and liquid hot
   pepper seasoning
1 teaspoon dill weed
3 bay leaves
2 sticks whole cinnamon
5 whole cloves
1 whole orange, thinly sliced

Put the corned beef in a Dutch oven; add 2 quarts water. Cover and bring to a boil, reduce heat, and simmer for 30 minutes. Taste water; if salty, discard and add 2 quarts more water to beef.

Stir in the onion, garlic powder, hot pepper seasoning, dill, bay, cinnamon, cloves, and orange slices. Cover and simmer for 2½ or 3 more hours or until meat is tender when pierced. Cool, cover, and chill overnight.

To serve, remove meat from broth (save it for a soup) and thinly slice meat across the grain. Makes 8 to 10 servings.

## Crusty Barbecued Beef

If you use a covered barbecue, follow the manufacturer's directions.

¼ cup each salad oil and apple juice
½ cup strong black coffee
1 tablespoon fennel seed
½ teaspoon onion powder
1 teaspoon salt
⅛ teaspoon pepper
5 to 6-pound cross rib beef roast, 5½ to 6½
   inches in diameter

Combine oil, apple juice, coffee, fennel, onion powder, salt, and pepper; pour over meat and let stand 1 to 2 hours, turning often.

Arrange a solid bed of hot glowing coals about 2 inches back from an imaginary line directly under the spit and 3 to 4 inches beyond either end of the meat. Add about 15 briquettes every 30 minutes to keep heat level constant. Run the spit through the center of roast; secure with spit forks. Insert a meat thermometer in thickest portion without touching spit. Position spit; surface of meat should be about 5 inches from surface of coals.

Set a shallow pan beneath meat to catch drippings. Cook, basting with marinade, until meat thermometer registers 135° for rare (about 2½ to 3 hours) or until done to your liking. Makes about 12 servings.

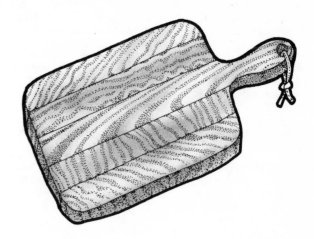

## Smoky Brisket, Oven-Style

Flavored by a smoky onion sauce, lean beef brisket bakes slowly to tenderness. It makes an inexpensive and easy-to-manage party entrée. You can prepare it and freeze half to serve later.

4½ to 5½-pound piece of lean beef brisket
1 tablespoon smoke-flavored salt
6 to 8 medium-sized onions, thinly sliced and
   separated into rings
1 cup (or 12 oz. bottle) tomato-based chile
   sauce
1 tablespoon celery seed
2 tablespoons mustard seed
½ teaspoon pepper

Sprinkle brisket with flavored salt and lay meat flat in a close-fitting pan (such as the bottom of a broiler pan). Bake, uncovered, in a 500° oven for 30 minutes, turning once, to brown lightly.

Remove from oven, lift meat out, and set aside; with a spoon, stir pan juices to free all browned bits. Arrange half the onions in an even layer in the pan bottom. Drizzle with half the chile sauce and sprinkle with half the celery seed, mustard seed, and pepper. Set the meat (adding any of the juices that may have drained from it) on the onions, then cover with remaining onions and top with remaining chile sauce, celery seed, mustard seed, and pepper.

Cover tightly (with heavy foil if you do not have a tight-fitting lid, folding foil snugly around the pan rim).

Bake in a 275° oven for 4 to 4½ hours or until meat is tender when pierced with a fork. Avoid hot steam when opening pan. (If the pan is not tightly sealed, the juices may evaporate and the meat scorch; if there is any indication that this is happening, add water to pan as needed to keep bottom slightly moist.)

Cover pan loosely and chill meat thoroughly (overnight, if convenient). Lift out meat and cut in ¼-inch-thick slices, going across the grain. Spread ¼ of the onions in each of 2 shallow pans or shallow casseroles—each 9 or 10 by 13 or 15 inches. Overlapping, arrange half the slices in each pan, covering onions. Then, in each pan, make a band of ¼ of the onions around edge of the meat. Add ½ of any juices to each pan.

(At this point you can cover the pans and refrigerate for several days or wrap for the freezer and freeze up to 2 weeks. Let thaw 12 to 24 hours in the refrigerator.) To reheat, cover pan tightly with a close-fitting lid or heavy foil and bake in a 375° oven for 35 to 45 minutes until hot throughout. Each pan serves 4 to 6; together, they serve 8 to 12.

## Sauerbraten

*The name in German means "sour or pickled beef," and it's a favorite dish that requires a few days to marinate.*

> *4 pounds beef rump, sirloin tip, or boned rolled lean chuck*
> *2 cups each cider vinegar and water*
> *2 large onions, peeled and sliced*
> *1 whole lemon, sliced*
> *10 whole cloves*
> *4 bay leaves*
> *6 whole black peppers*
> *2 tablespoons each salt and sugar*
> *All-purpose flour*
> *2 tablespoons salad oil*
> *About ½ cup water*
> *8 gingersnaps*
> *2 tablespoons all-purpose flour*

Place meat in a deep glass or ceramic bowl. Combine vinegar, the 2 cups water, onions, lemon, cloves, bay leaves, pepper, salt, and sugar; pour over meat, cover, and refrigerate for 36 to 48 hours; turn 3 or 4 times to season evenly.

Remove meat from vinegar mixture and rub surface lightly with flour (about 2 tablespoons in all); reserve 1 cup of the marinade. Heat oil in a heavy frying pan or roaster that has a cover. Brown meat on all sides, add the reserved 1 cup vinegar mixture and the ½ cup water. Cover tightly and cook in a 350° oven for 2 to 2½ hours

or until meat is tender. Remove to a serving platter.

Strain the meat juices and add water, if needed, to make 2 cups liquid. Bring to boil over medium heat. Crush the gingersnaps and combine with the 2 tablespoons flour, stirring into the juices; cook until thickened. Serve in a bowl to spoon over meat slices. Makes about 8 servings.

## Giant Meatball

*Shaped like a giant meatball, this spicy meatloaf is based on a discovery from Istanbul. Lamb, oregano, spices, and pine nuts give it Middle-Eastern identification.*

> *2 tablespoons butter or margarine*
> *1 medium-sized onion, finely chopped*
> *½ cup fine, dry bread crumbs*
> *¼ cup dry red wine or tomato juice*
> *1½ teaspoons salt*
> *½ teaspoon oregano leaves, crumbled*
> *¼ teaspoon each pepper, ground cinnamon, and ground nutmeg*
> *⅓ cup finely chopped parsley*
> *2 eggs*
> *2 pounds lean ground lamb*
> *⅓ cup pine nuts*
> *Parsley sprigs*
> *Lemon wedges*
> *About 1 carton (8 oz.) unflavored yogurt*

In a frying pan, melt the butter over medium-high heat; add the onion and cook, stirring, until limp (about 5 minutes); turn into a large bowl. Add to the bowl the bread crumbs, wine, salt, oregano, pepper, cinnamon, nutmeg, chopped parsley, eggs, and ground lamb, mixing well.

Use your hands to form meat into a large compact ball. Roll in pine nuts, pressing them into the meat. Set the meatball in a pie pan and bake in a 325° oven for 1½ hours or until nuts become golden. Transfer to a serving plate and garnish with parsley sprigs and lemon. To serve, cut in wedges and offer yogurt to spoon over the meat like a sauce. Makes about 6 servings.

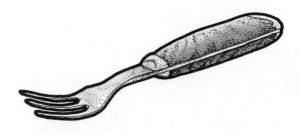

# Meatballs Menthe

Mint imparts a delicate, fresh flavor to these meatballs, which are two-thirds beef and one-third lamb.

    1 pound lean ground beef
    ½ pound lean ground lamb
    1½ tablespoons finely chopped fresh mint
    ½ cup fresh bread crumbs
    2 eggs
    1 medium-sized onion, finely chopped
    1¼ teaspoons salt
    ⅛ teaspoon pepper
      All-purpose flour
    6 tablespoons salad oil
    1 can (1 lb.) tomatoes
    ½ teaspoon basil leaves
      Salt and pepper

Mix the ground beef and lamb or have your meat man grind both meats together. Wash and finely chop mint leaves and stems and add 1 tablespoon to the meat mixture together with the bread crumbs, eggs, onion, salt, and pepper. Blend and shape into balls about 1½ inches in diameter, rolling the balls in flour. Heat the oil in a frying pan or electric frying pan and brown the meatballs, turning frequently.

When meatballs are well browned, pour off excess fat and add tomatoes, basil, remaining ½ tablespoon mint, salt and pepper to taste. Cover and cook 15 minutes. Makes about 4 to 6 servings.

# Herbed Leg of Lamb

Herbs and mustard flavor this leg of lamb roast. Garlic slivers are inserted in slits under the skin.

    5½ to 6-pound leg of lamb
    2 cloves garlic
    1 tablespoon dry mustard
    1 teaspoon salt
    ⅛ teaspoon pepper
    ½ teaspoon thyme leaves
    ¼ teaspoon crushed rosemary leaves
    1 tablespoon lemon juice
      Water
    2 tablespoons all-purpose flour

Rub all surfaces of the lamb with one of the garlic cloves, peeled and halved. Cut both cloves into slivers. Slit skin of lamb at intervals over the top surface; insert slivered garlic into slits. Blend the mustard, salt, pepper, thyme, rosemary, and lemon juice. Spread over surface of the roast.

Place lamb on a rack in an uncovered roasting pan and put into a 325° oven. Roast for 2 to 2½ hours (longer for medium or well done). Roast until a meat thermometer inserted in thickest part registers 150° for medium-rare, 160° for medium-well done, or 175° for well done.

Remove meat to a platter and keep warm. Pour pan drippings into a pint measure and skim off fat, reserving 2 tablespoons. Add water to drippings to make 1½ cups liquid; pour it back into roasting pan and heat to stir up the brown bits; set aside. In a saucepan blend the 2 tablespoons reserved fat with the flour; cook, stirring, until bubbly. Remove from heat and gradually add the pan liquid. Cook, stirring, until it boils and thickens; serve with the roast. Makes 6 to 8 servings.

# Lamb Curry

Check your spice supply before starting this curry, but don't be concerned that it will turn out overly spicy. The end product is smooth and exotic.

    2 medium-sized onions
    2 cloves garlic
    2 tablespoons ground coriander
    2 teaspoons each salt and cumin seed
    1½ teaspoons each black pepper, ground cloves,
        and ground cardamom
    1 teaspoon each ground ginger, ground
        cinnamon, and poppy seed
    ⅓ cup lemon juice
    2 cups unflavored yogurt
    5 pounds boneless lamb, cut in 1½-inch cubes
    ¼ cup (⅛ lb.) butter or margarine
      Curry powder (optional)

Cut 1 of the onions and 1 clove of the garlic directly into an electric blender. (If you don't have a blender, grate the onion and mash the garlic and combine in a bowl.) Add the coriander, salt, cumin, pepper, cloves, cardamom, ginger, cinnamon, poppy seed, and lemon juice; whirl or beat until smooth and thoroughly blended. Blend in the yogurt. Pour this sauce over the meat in a large container, stirring until all the meat pieces are coated. Cover and let stand 1 to 2 hours at room temperature or overnight in the refrigerator.

Melt the butter in a large frying pan or other heavy pan; thinly slice the remaining onion and 1 clove garlic, and sauté in the butter until golden. Add the meat, including the marinating sauce. Cover and simmer slowly until the lamb is tender (about 2 hours). This makes quite a mild curry, so taste and add prepared curry powder (we used about 3 teaspoons) if you want to increase the curry spiciness. Makes about 12 servings.

## Lamb Chops, Mexican-Style

The meat goes first into an herb-garlic-oil marinade, then is coated with a nippy red sauce and grilled, Mexican-style.

½ cup olive oil or salad oil
2 tablespoons rosemary leaves, crumbled
2 teaspoons garlic powder
1 tablespoon oregano leaves, crumbled
8 lamb shoulder chops, each cut about 1 inch thick
1 cup prepared taco sauce
½ cup (¼ lb.) butter or margarine
½ cup catsup
¼ cup wine vinegar

In a wide pan, blend the oil with the rosemary, garlic powder, and oregano. Turn the lamb chops into this herb-oil mixture; cover and let stand in a cool place for several hours. Rotate chops occasionally to marinate evenly.

In a small pan, heat together the taco sauce, butter, catsup, and vinegar until the butter is melted. Dip the chops, one at a time, in sauce to coat all sides. Place immediately on the grill about 5 inches above hot coals. Cook until done to stage you prefer (about 10 minutes to a side for medium-rare).

Baste meat once with the hot sauce after turning. Reheat sauce, and serve to spoon over chops. Makes 4 to 8 servings.

## Baked Lamb Stew with Yams

From the West Indies comes this stew reflecting their characteristic seasonings and interesting combinations of fruits and vegetables. The bananas used must be green all over; used this way, they resemble potatoes and take about the same length of time to cook.

2½ pounds boneless lamb stew meat cut in 1½-inch cubes
2 medium-sized onions, chopped
1 or 2 cloves garlic, minced or mashed
1½ teaspoons ground coriander
1 teaspoon oregano leaves
½ teaspoon ground cumin
¼ teaspoon each ground ginger and cloves
2 tablespoons soy sauce
1 cup hot water
6 to 8 medium-sized yams or sweet potatoes
6 medium-sized carrots
3 green bananas
¼ cup all-purpose flour
1 can (14½ oz.) pear shaped tomatoes
Salt and pepper to taste

Put the meat into a baking dish or casserole (about 9 by 13 inches). Distribute the onion and garlic around the meat in the dish. Sprinkle with coriander, oregano, cumin, ginger, and cloves. Drizzle with soy, then pour the water over. Cover tightly with foil or a lid and bake in a 425° oven for 1½ hours. After about 1¼ hours, put the yams into the oven around the casserole.

Meanwhile, peel carrots and cut into thick diagonal slices. Score the bananas, peel, and cut into chunks about the same size as carrots.

Remove meat from oven after 1½ hours cooking and stir in flour, blended smooth with some of the tomato liquid. Add the tomatoes and remaining liquid, carrots, and bananas; stir to distribute evenly. Cover dish again and continue baking for about 30 minutes or until meat and vegetables in the stew are tender and yams are baked.

Taste the stew and correct seasoning with salt and pepper, if needed. Transfer to a serving dish or bring to the table in the casserole. Pass the baked yams separately to eat, spooning over them some of the flavorful juices from the stew. Makes 6 to 8 servings.

## Portuguese-Style Barbecued Lamb Chops

Here is a choice of two red wine and oil marinades. Both result in exceptionally juicy, tender chops. Marinate chops overnight, then use sauce generously for basting the meat while it grills.

In a large shallow baking dish, prepare either the Cumin-Cinnamon Marinade or Pickling Spice Marinade (recipes, page 42). Put 5 or 6 shoulder lamb chops (about 3 lbs.), each cut about ¾ inch thick, into the marinade, turn to wet all sides, then arrange in a single layer. Cover and refrigerate at least 8 hours or overnight. Turn chops over in the marinade occasionally.

*(Continued on next page)*

Lift chops from marinade and drain, reserving marinade. Arrange chops on a barbecue grill about 6 inches above a medium-hot fire of about 30 fully ignited coals.

Grill chops about 15 minutes on each side or until meat is light pink inside (cut a gash in the meat to check); occasionally turn chops over and frequently baste both sides with marinade. Makes 5 to 6 servings.

### Cumin-Cinnamon Marinade

1 cup dry red wine
¼ cup olive oil or salad oil
3 cloves garlic, minced or mashed
1 teaspoon each salt and ground cumin seed
¾ teaspoon ground cinnamon
⅓ cup finely chopped onion
1 tablespoon cumin seed

In a shallow baking pan, combine the wine, olive oil, garlic, salt, ground cumin, cinnamon, onion, and cumin seed. Stir to mix, then use to marinate shoulder lamb chops as directed on page 41.

### Picking Spice Marinade

1 cup dry red wine
¼ cup each salad oil and wine vinegar
2 cloves garlic, minced or mashed
1 teaspoon salt
½ cup chopped onion
1 tablespoon whole mixed pickling spice
4 whole cloves
¼ teaspoon ground cloves

In a large shallow baking dish, combine the wine, oil, vinegar, garlic, salt, onion, pickling spice, whole cloves, and ground cloves. Stir to mix. Use as directed on page 41.

## Moroccan Lamb Stew

Dried apricots, lemon, honey, sweet spices, and fresh coriander deliciously season this stew from Morocco.

3 tablespoons each olive oil and butter
2 medium-sized onions, thinly sliced
1¼ teaspoons salt
2 teaspoons ground ginger
¼ teaspoon pepper
3 sticks whole cinnamon
3½ pounds boneless lamb leg, cut in 1½-inch cubes (about 1 small leg)
1 cup moist dried apricots
About 1 bunch fresh coriander
2 tablespoons honey
1½ tablespoons lemon juice
¼ cup sesame seed, toasted

In a heavy Dutch oven, heat the olive oil and butter. Add onions, salt, ginger, pepper, and cinnamon; cook, stirring, about 3 minutes. Add the meat and mix to coat with the onion mixture. Cover and simmer gently until the meat is tender (about 1½ hours). Turn the meat occasionally, adding a little water if needed to prevent sticking. Stir in the apricots. Trim coriander and tie about 6 of the plants together with cord. Put in on top of meat; cover and cook until apricots are tender (about 5 minutes).

Remove from heat and discard coriander. With a slotted spoon, remove meat and apricots to a serving plate and keep warm. Stir honey into pan juices and boil if needed to reduce and thicken the juices. Stir in lemon juice and pour over the meat. Coarsely chop remaining coriander and pass with sesame seed at the table to sprinkle on top. Makes about 6 servings.

## How to Make Fresh Horseradish

Pure horseradish made from the fresh root is very hot. Our recipe blends horseradish with some turnip to temper the heat slightly, but you can make it milder by increasing the amount of turnip you use. Even so, it is important to prepare horseradish in an electric blender as the blender's cover protects the cook from the eye-watering fumes that rise from the cut surfaces of the horseradish.

Some markets that specialize in fresh produce carry the horseradish root; others will order it on request. A 1-pound root will make about 3 cups of prepared horseradish. It can be refrigerated up to three months or frozen.

1 horseradish root (about 1 lb.)
1 cup white vinegar
1 teaspoon salt
½ teaspoon sugar
1 small turnip, peeled and cubed

Scrub and peel horseradish root, cutting away dark parts. Cut into cubes (you should have about 3 cups). Place vinegar, salt, and sugar in blender container. Add about ⅓ each of the horseradish and turnip. Whirl until smooth, occasionally removing cover, and stirring down from sides. Add remaining horseradish and turnip gradually, blending until vegetables are uniformly grated. Makes about 3 cups.

## Country-Style Spareribs in Garlic Wine

Of Portuguese origin is this variation of *vinha d' alhos*, or garlic wine. Meaty country-style spareribs marinate for several days in a mild, aromatic garlic wine. Use whole coriander and cumin seeds; crush them with a mortar and pestle, blender, or rolling pin.

*4 pounds country-style spareribs*
*1 cup cider vinegar*
*3 cups water*
*½ cup dry white table wine*
*2 teaspoons each coriander and cumin seed,*
*    crushed*
*5 to 6 whole garlic cloves, crushed slightly*
*¼ teaspoon cayenne*
*2 teaspoons salt*
*    Water*
*    Salt to taste*

Put the spareribs in a deep glass bowl or ceramic bowl. Blend together the vinegar, 3 cups water, wine, coriander, cumin, garlic, cayenne, and 2 teaspoons salt. Pour liquid over pork. Cover bowl and refrigerate for 4 days; turn meat in marinade several times during this period.

On the fourth day, remove meat from marinade and let drain for about 30 minutes. Discard all liquid. Arrange meat in single layer in roasting pan and add ½ cup water. Bake, uncovered, in a 350° oven for 2 hours. Remove meat to a serving platter. Skim as much fat as possible from drippings, then add 4 to 6 tablespoons water to pan and bring to a boil, scraping free all the browned particles. Serve separately in a sauce dish. Cut between ribs to serve meat; it may require additional salt to taste. Makes 4 servings.

## Baked Ham with Caraway Honey Glaze

You can serve the ham either hot or cold. Serve as a main dish or slice and assemble sandwiches, spreading bread with Cheddar cheese spread and topping with ham and pickles.

*5 or 6-pound bone-in ham (butt or shank end)*
*    or a canned ham*
*2 tablespoons honey*
*1 teaspoon prepared mustard*
*½ teaspoon caraway seed*

Bake ham in a 325° oven for about 1½ to 2 hours or until hot throughout (heat canned ham as directed on can). Remove from oven and score the top in a diamond pattern with a sharp knife. Mix the honey, mustard, and caraway seed together; spread over ham. Bake for 15 minutes longer or until glaze melts. A 5-pound ham serves 8 to 10.

## Spiced Pork Roll

Once cooked, the roll keeps well in the refrigerator for about a week, ready to serve. The Green Herbed Mayonnaise can be served as a sauce for the meat or spread on bread for sandwiches.

*5-pound pork loin end roast, boned*
*½ teaspoon each ground allspice, ground pepper,*
*    and sugar*
*1 teaspoon salt*
*6 to 8 whole cloves*
*4 cups water*
*2 carrots, sliced*
*1 onion, sliced*
*8 to 10 each whole black peppers and whole*
*    allspice*
*    Green Herbed Mayonnaise (recipe follows)*

Trim and discard as much fat as possible from meat. Mix ground allspice, pepper, sugar, salt; rub into all sides of meat.

Form meat into a compact loaf shape and tie securely at 1-inch intervals crosswise and lengthwise. Stud the meat with cloves. Set roll in the bottom of a 4 or 5-quart pan; add water, carrots, onion, whole peppers and allspice. Bring to a boil, cover, and simmer 1½ hours; turn meat over once or twice while cooking.

Remove pan from heat, place a flat plate (or pie pan) directly on meat, and set a heavy weight such as a brick on the plate. Chill thoroughly. Remove meat from broth (save broth for soup or other uses) and cut away all the string. Wrap in clear plastic film and keep in the refrigerator up to 7 days. Slice meat thinly. Makes 10 to 12 servings.

*Green Herbed Mayonnaise.* In a blender jar, combine ¼ cup chopped, lightly packed parsley, ¼ cup chopped fresh, frozen or freeze-dried chives, ¼ teaspoon dill weed, 4 teaspoons lemon juice, and ½ cup mayonnaise. Cover jar and whirl mixture until smoothly blended and pale green in color. Cover and chill until serving time. Makes about ½ cup.

## Caraway Pork Chops

The pan drippings from these tender, zesty chops give a rich, flavorful base for gravy.

6 pork chops
¼ cup all-purpose flour
½ teaspoon salt
⅛ teaspoon pepper
2 tablespoons salad oil
1 cup hot water
1½ teaspoons caraway seed
All-purpose flour

Roll the pork chops in a mixture of the flour, salt, and pepper. In a wide frying pan (one with a tight fitting lid) over medium-high heat, brown the chops on both sides in the oil, draining off excess fat as it accumulates. Add the hot water and caraway seed and cover pan tightly. Reduce heat and simmer for about 30 minutes. Remove lid during the last 5 minutes of cooking to evaporate most of the liquid; serve this unthickened gravy with meat. Or add flour and liquid to the drippings to make a thickened gravy.

## Spicy Spareribs

Chile powder is the identifiable flavoring accent in this zestful recipe.

½ cup sugar
1 cup each vinegar and water
½ teaspoon each chile powder and ground allspice
1 large onion, chopped
¾ cup catsup
2 tablespoons meat seasoning sauce
2 teaspoons salt
Dash liquid smoke
3 pounds spareribs

In a pan mix together until blended the sugar, vinegar, water, chile powder, allspice, onion, catsup, meat seasoning sauce, salt, and liquid smoke. Cut spareribs into serving-sized pieces and place in the pan with the sauce. Bring to a boil and simmer for 30 minutes, turning ribs occasionally. Remove ribs from sauce and place in a single layer in a shallow baking pan. Skim off fat from sauce and baste meat with some of the sauce.

Bake in a 350° oven for 30 minutes or until tender; turn ribs and baste occasionally with the remaining sauce. Broil ribs about 5 minutes to finish browning. Or, if you wish, barbecue the parboiled ribs over hot coals for about 30 minutes, turning occasionally and basting with the sauce

only during the last 15 minutes of cooking; cook until glazed and tender. Makes 4 servings.

## Spicy Italian Patties

These pork patties taste much like Italian sausages. Try serving them with hot garlic bread and a mixed green salad.

1 pound lean ground pork
¼ cup fine dry bread crumbs
1 egg
2 cloves garlic, minced or mashed
2 tablespoons dry red wine
½ teaspoon each salt, pepper, and fennel or anise seed
Salad oil for pan broiling

Mix together the pork, crumbs, egg, garlic, wine, salt, pepper, and fennel seed. Divide into 4 equal-sized portions and shape into patties about ½-inch thick. If you pan broil the patties, heat 1 tablespoon salad oil in a 10-inch frying pan over medium-low heat for 1 minute. Lay the patties in the pan and cook 6 to 7 minutes on each side or until meat is no longer pink inside. If you broil the patties, place them on a broiler rack about 4 inches from the heat and cook about 6 minutes on each side. Makes 4 servings.

# Guide to Prepared Mustard

If you browse through the shelves of a specialty food store or delicatessen, you'll find mustards from around the world. And they come in all types of containers from tubes to crockery jars.

Prepared mustards are made of a basic mixture of dry mustard, vinegar, and seasonings. They get their distinct and varying flavors from added vinegars, wines, horseradish, sugar, herbs or other seasonings. Some are colored a vivid yellow with the addition of turmeric; others are left with a natural pale yellow or brownish shade.

Mustards can be sweet to sharp, winy, biting, mild, hot, pungent, musty, or tangy. Your mustard choice will be a matter of personal preference.

Generally, the lightly colored mustards are mild in flavor and best complement lightly seasoned foods. Dark mustards are usually heavier in flavor and complement robust dishes.

## Mustard Styles

Mustards tend to reflect the foods of the country of their origin. Dijon mustard (named for a town in eastern France known for its mustard) has become the term used for typical French mustards.

*French mustards* are delicately flavored to complement the carefully blended French seasonings used in foods. This light gold condiment has white wine as the liquid ingredient. Used in very small amounts, it is subtly delicious on almost everything. Our domestic Dijon mustard is a bit less potent than the native form.

*English mustards* have a clear vinegar aroma and extreme sharpness, yet come across with sweetness. They blend well with bland foods that can take a slightly sweet mustard flavor—ham, pork, mild cheese, fish, or highly flavored meats.

*German mustards* are dark tan, lusty, and musty. Use with foods having a strong character of their own, or you'll taste nothing but the mustard. Try it on German or Polish sausages or sauerkraut.

*Dutch mustards* are strong and sour; color may vary from light pinkish brown to dark brown. Try it on corned beef and brockwurst.

*Swedish mustards* are smooth but tangy, a natural smörgåsbord choice to go with many different food choices. They do vary in flavor from domestic and imported varieties.

Of course the countries producing mustards go beyond these, and include herb flavored blends, combinations of horseradish, wines, and champagnes. But those listed above will familiarize you with a few more available varieties.

## Homemade Mustard

You begin with dry mustard, adding vinegar for tartness and wine for mellowness, then cook with egg yolks to make a velvety smooth spread. You can season the mildly flavored mustard as suggested or leave it plain to serve as you would any prepared mustard.

In the top of a double boiler blend $\frac{1}{4}$ cup *each* dry mustard and white wine vinegar, $\frac{1}{3}$ cup dry white wine, 1 tablespoon sugar, and $\frac{1}{2}$ teaspoon salt. Let stand, uncovered, for 2 hours.

Beat 3 egg yolks into mustard mixture. Cook, stirring constantly with a wire whip, over hot (not boiling) water until as thick as softly whipped cream; about 5 minutes. Pour into small jars and cool. Cover tightly and store in the refrigerator up to 1 month. Makes about 1 cup.

**Lime Mustard.** When you remove mustard from heat, stir in $\frac{3}{4}$ teaspoon grated lime peel and $1\frac{1}{2}$ teaspoons lime juice. Serve with roast lamb or chicken, shrimp, or sautéed fish.

**Tarragon Mustard.** When you remove mustard from heat, stir in $\frac{1}{2}$ teaspoon crushed tarragon leaves. Serve with roast lamb or chicken, shrimp, steaks, or as a sandwich spread.

**Spicy Mustard.** When you beat egg yolks into mustard, also add $\frac{1}{4}$ teaspoon *each* ground turmeric and cloves. Serve with baked ham, on meat sandwiches, on hamburgers or frankfurters.

**Tomato Mustard.** When you beat egg yolks into mustard, also add 1 teaspoon paprika, 1 tablespoon drained and chopped pimiento, and $\frac{1}{4}$ cup canned tomato paste. Serve with shrimp, sautéed fish, hamburgers or frankfurters, or with baked ham.

# Poultry

## Perking Up Chicken and Turkey

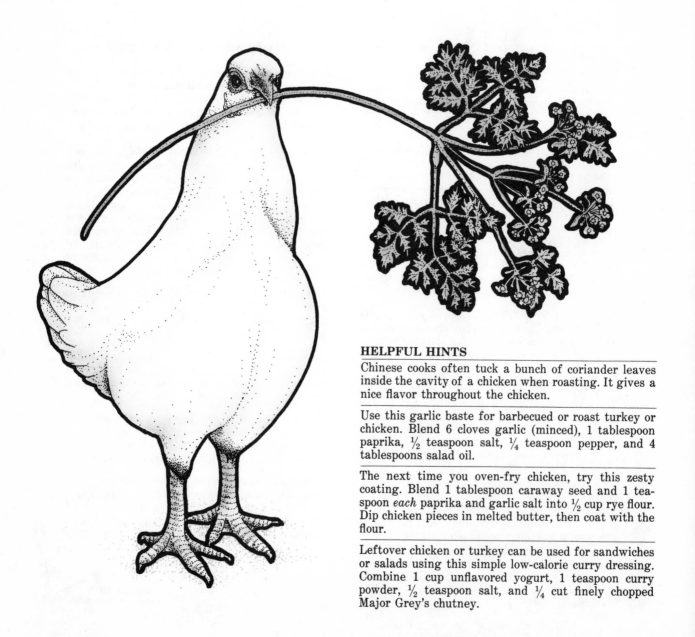

### HELPFUL HINTS

Chinese cooks often tuck a bunch of coriander leaves inside the cavity of a chicken when roasting. It gives a nice flavor throughout the chicken.

Use this garlic baste for barbecued or roast turkey or chicken. Blend 6 cloves garlic (minced), 1 tablespoon paprika, ½ teaspoon salt, ¼ teaspoon pepper, and 4 tablespoons salad oil.

The next time you oven-fry chicken, try this zesty coating. Blend 1 tablespoon caraway seed and 1 teaspoon *each* paprika and garlic salt into ½ cup rye flour. Dip chicken pieces in melted butter, then coat with the flour.

Leftover chicken or turkey can be used for sandwiches or salads using this simple low-calorie curry dressing. Combine 1 cup unflavored yogurt, 1 teaspoon curry powder, ½ teaspoon salt, and ¼ cut finely chopped Major Grey's chutney.

# Chicken with Basil

Basil is popular in the cuisine of Thailand. Often it is combined with hot chiles to produce an interesting flavor contrast.

3 to 4 tablespoons finely chopped canned
    California green chiles, seeded
2 tablespoons soy sauce
1 teaspoon each sugar and vinegar
½ cup coarsely chopped fresh basil leaves or
    2 tablespoons dried basil leaves
1 teaspoon chopped fresh or dried mint leaves
½ teaspoon cornstarch
3 tablespoons salad oil
2 whole chicken breasts (about 1 lb. each),
    skinned, boned, and cut in strips ¼ inch
    thick and 2 inches long
1 clove garlic, minced or mashed
1 large onion, halved, then sliced ¼ inch thick

Mix together chiles, soy, sugar, vinegar, basil, mint, and cornstarch; set aside.

Heat 2 tablespoons of the oil in a large frying pan or wok over high heat. When oil is hot, add the chicken and garlic; cook, stirring constantly, until meat loses pinkness (about 4 minutes); then turn out of pan. Heat another 1 tablespoon oil, then add onion; cook, stirring, for 1 minute. Add chile mixture and return chicken and juices to pan; cook, stirring, until sauce thickens slightly. Makes 3 or 4 servings.

# Chicken with Coriander Onion

Coriander seasons the slow-cooked onions that dress this El Salvador-style chicken dish. You might buy barbecued chicken from the market or broil, bake, or barbecue chicken halves or quarters at home.

4 tablespoons butter or margarine
4 large onions, thinly sliced
1 can (8 oz.) tomato sauce
1 tablespoon Worcestershire
1 tablespoon finely chopped fresh coriander or
    ½ teaspoon dried coriander leaves, crumbled
    or ¼ teaspoon ground coriander
    Hot, cooked chicken halves or quarters for
    4 to 6 servings

In a 10-inch frying pan over medium heat, melt the butter; add onions and sauté, stirring often, until golden (about 20 minutes). Stir in the tomato sauce, Worcestershire, and coriander; bring to boiling. (At this point you can cover and refrigerate the onions; then reheat shortly before serving.)

At serving time arrange hot chicken on a serving platter and spoon the onions over the top. Makes 4 to 6 servings.

# Barbecued Chicken Provençal

Herbs, garlic, and mustard coat chicken legs and thighs grilled over the coals until a crisp skin develops.

3 pounds broiler-fryer legs and thighs, joined
2 tablespoons Dijon mustard
2 teaspoons dry white wine or lemon juice
1 teaspoon Italian herb seasoning or ¼ teaspoon
    each basil, oregano, rosemary, and thyme
    leaves
1 teaspoon instant minced onion
1 clove garlic, minced or mashed

Rinse chicken and pat dry. In a small bowl, mix mustard, wine, herb seasoning, onion, and garlic until smooth. Spread the mustard mixture evenly over all sides of chicken pieces. Cover lightly and refrigerate for 2 to 4 hours.

Arrange chicken on a barbecue grill about 6 inches above low glowing coals. Grill until well browned on all sides and meat near bone is no longer pink (about 45 minutes). Makes 4 servings.

# Chinese Five-Spice Chicken

The Chinese often blend several spices, using them in small amounts to flavor foods. One such combination, available in most Oriental stores and some supermarkets, is simply called Chinese five-spice. A similar blend of spices is used in the recipe below. You could omit the ginger, cinnamon, allspice, anise, and clove in the recipe and use 2 teaspoons Chinese five-spice.

3 to 4-pound broiler-fryer, cut into serving
    pieces
½ cup soy sauce
¼ cup chopped onion
1 clove garlic, crushed
1 teaspoon minced fresh ginger
½ teaspoon ground cinnamon
¼ teaspoon each ground allspice and crushed
    anise seed
⅛ teaspoon ground cloves
    Dash black pepper

In a glass or ceramic bowl, marinate the chicken pieces in the soy sauce mixed with the onion, garlic, and ginger for 3 to 4 hours. Drain and arrange chicken in a shallow, greased, 9 by 13-inch baking pan. Mix the cinnamon, allspice, anise, cloves, and pepper; sprinkle over chicken and bake in a 325° oven for about 1 hour or until tender, turning once. Makes 4 servings.

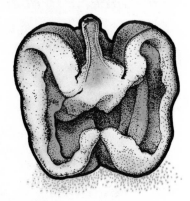

## Spicy Oven-Fried Chicken

Curry and other spices flavor chicken quarters and develop a rich brown glaze while the pieces oven-fry.

1 large broiler-fryer chicken (3 to 3½ lbs.),
    quartered
½ teaspoon salt
6 tablespoons butter or margarine
2 teaspoons Worcestershire
2 teaspoons curry powder
1 teaspoon oregano leaves, crumbled
½ teaspoon each dry mustard and garlic powder
¼ teaspoon paprika
3 dashes liquid hot pepper seasoning
1 chicken bouillon cube or 1 teaspoon chicken
    stock base

Wash chicken pieces and pat dry. Sprinkle with salt and arrange skin side down in a 9 by 13-inch baking pan.

In a small saucepan, melt the butter, then blend in Worcestershire, curry powder, oregano, mustard, garlic powder, paprika, liquid hot pepper seasoning, and the bouillon cube or chicken stock base. Brush the sauce generously over the chicken pieces. Bake, uncovered, in a 375° oven for about 20 minutes.

Turn the chicken pieces skin side up, again brush them generously with the butter mixture, and continue baking until the chicken is tender and nicely browned (about 40 to 50 minutes total baking time). Baste once or twice more with the butter mixture, using it all by the time the chicken is done.

Remove the cooked chicken to a warm serving platter and drizzle it with the butter sauce from the baking pan. Makes 4 servings.

## Chile Chicken Sauté

About an hour before you plan to serve it, brown the chicken, then let it simmer, unattended, in a spicy tomato sauce.

1 large onion, thinly sliced
5 tablespoons butter or margarine
2 cloves garlic, minced or mashed
1 large broiler-fryer chicken (about 3 lbs.),
    cut up
¼ cup all-purpose flour
1 large can (1 lb. 12 oz.) pear shaped tomatoes
2 tablespoons firmly packed brown sugar
1 tablespoon chile powder
¼ teaspoon ground cinnamon
1 green pepper, seeded and sliced in rings

In a large frying pan or Dutch oven, sauté onion in 2 tablespoons of the butter until limp; add the garlic and stir until very lightly browned. Transfer onion and garlic with a slotted spoon to a small bowl, then set aside. Dredge chicken pieces in flour and shake off excess. Add remaining 3 tablespoons butter to the pan and brown chicken over medium heat. Remove chicken breast; set aside.

Drain tomatoes, reserving ¾ cup of the liquid. Coarsely chop tomatoes and add to chicken. Stir the brown sugar, chile powder, and cinnamon into reserved tomato liquid; pour over chicken. Return onion and garlic to pan. Turn heat to low, cover, and simmer until chicken is tender when pierced with a fork (about 20 minutes); add chicken breast the last 10 minutes.

Transfer chicken to a serving dish; keep warm. Add green pepper ring to pan. Turn heat to high and boil, stirring to reduce liquid by about one third; pour over chicken. Makes 4 servings.

## Chicken Sautéed with Shallots

Shallots and herbs combine with butter and white wine to produce a succulent chicken dish.

3-pound broiler-fryer, cut into serving pieces
1 teaspoon salt
¼ cup butter or margarine
¼ cup finely chopped shallots
½ teaspoon tarragon leaves
2 teaspoons minced parsley
1 teaspoon chervil leaves
1 cup dry white wine
    Parsley sprigs or watercress

Sprinkle the chicken pieces with salt. Melt butter in a wide frying pan and brown chicken pieces on all sides. Move some of the browned chicken to one side of the pan; into the empty area put the shallots, tarragon, parsley, and chervil. Cook about 5 minutes over medium heat or until shallots are lightly browned and slightly soft. Gently shake the pan to distribute the shallots and herbs among the chicken pieces. Pour the white wine into the pan. Cover and simmer gently for about 30 minutes or until the chicken is tender when pierced. Transfer chicken pieces to a warm serving dish. Skim fat from pan juices, then pour juices over chicken. Garnish with parsley sprigs or watercress. Makes 4 servings.

## Island Chicken

Grill marinated chicken pieces over low glowing coals, turning and basting often. Some of the marinade is thickened to make a sauce for the chicken and rice.

⅓ cup soy sauce
1 cup water
1 clove garlic, minced or mashed
1 tablespoon sugar
2 tablespoons dry Sherry or lemon juice
3 tablespoons grated fresh ginger (or 1 teaspoon ground ginger)
3 to 3½-pound broiler-fryer chicken, quartered
¼ cup sesame seed
2 teaspoons each cornstarch and water
   Hot, cooked rice

Combine the soy, water, garlic, sugar, Sherry, and ginger and pour over chicken. Cover and chill at least 4 hours or overnight, turning often.

To barbecue, lift chicken from marinade and drain briefly; place on a grill about 6 inches above a bed of low, glowing coals. Grill until browned on all sides and meat near bone is no longer pink (about 45 minutes); baste with ⅓ cup of the marinade.

Toast sesame seed in a frying pan over medium heat, stirring until golden. Pour in remaining 1 cup marinade; blend cornstarch and water, stir into pan; cook, stirring, until thickened; spoon over chicken and rice. Serves 4.

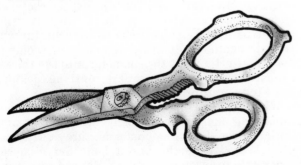

## Barbecued Sweet-Sour Chicken

First cook chicken pieces in the marinade, allowing it to absorb the flavors. Then it is easily glazed to a rich brown while heating on the barbecue.

4 each chicken legs and thighs or
   1 broiler-fryer chicken, cut up
⅓ cup each lemon juice and mild honey
½ cup dry white wine or apple juice
2 tablespoons Worcestershire
3 tablespoons Dijon mustard
½ teaspoon salt
¼ teaspoon basil leaves
¼ teaspoon liquid hot pepper seasoning

Rinse chicken pieces and pat dry. In a Dutch oven, combine the lemon juice, honey, wine, Worcestershire, mustard, salt, basil, and hot pepper seasoning. Bring to a boil, put in chicken pieces, reduce heat, cover, and simmer gently until chicken is tender (about 20 minutes). Remove from heat and let stand for at least 30 minutes or up to 3 hours.

To barbecue, remove chicken from marinade and arrange on the grill over low glowing coals. Watch carefully and turn often until browned and heated through, basting with the marinade. Makes about 4 servings.

## Sautéed Chicken with Artichokes

The subtle flavors of anise seed, thyme, and smoked ham permeate the chicken in this recipe. Artichoke hearts are added during the last few minutes of cooking.

1 broiler-fryer chicken, cut up
2 tablespoons butter, margarine, or salad oil
¼ cup (about ¼ lb.) diced cooked ham
½ cup chopped onions
1 tablespoon chopped pimiento
2 teaspoons tomato paste or catsup
1 teaspoon each anise seed and salt
¼ teaspoon thyme leaves
   Dash pepper
½ cup each regular strength chicken broth and
   dry white wine (or 1 cup chicken broth)
1 package (10 oz.) frozen artichoke hearts
   Parsley for garnish

Wash and dry chicken thoroughly. Heat butter, margarine, or salad oil in large frying pan and brown chicken on all sides. Then add ham, onions, pimiento, tomato paste or catsup, anise seed, salt, thyme, pepper, chicken broth, and wine. Cover and simmer about 20 minutes. Add artichoke hearts, cover, and simmer 10 minutes or until chicken and artichokes are just tender; remove them to warm platter and keep warm. Boil liquid rapidly until reduced and slightly thickened; pour over chicken. Garnish with parsley. Makes 4 servings.

## Barbecued Turkey with Onion Stuffing, Lemon-Sherry Gravy

An impressive, easy way to cook turkey is to roast it on the barbecue stuffed with little onions and basted with a lemon-Sherry combination that is also used as the base for the gravy.

Start charcoal about 4½ to 5 hours before serving, allowing 3½ to 4 hours cooking and ½ hour for turkey to "rest" before carving.

1¼ to 1½ pounds small whole boiling onions
    Water
¼ cup melted butter
1 teaspoon each salt and grated lemon peel
½ teaspoon thyme leaves
10 to 12-pound turkey, fresh or thawed
1 cup melted butter
¼ cup dry Sherry
2 tablespoons lemon juice
¼ teaspoon dry mustard
½ teaspoon salt
    Regular strength chicken broth
½ cup all-purpose flour
    Salt and pepper

Peel and boil onions in water until tender (about 15 minutes); drain. Mix the ¼ cup melted butter, the 1 teaspoon salt, lemon peel, and thyme leaves. Let cool thoroughly. Cover and chill, if made ahead.

Rinse turkey and pat dry. Stuff cold onion mixture into turkey cavity and pin neck skin to back with skewers; skewer body opening shut. Run spit through neck and body opening of turkey. Center and hold in place with spit forks in breast and thighs; tie wings and legs securely to body. Insert meat thermometer into thickest part of breast.

To prepare the basting sauce, stir together the 1 cup melted butter, Sherry, lemon juice, dry mustard, and ½ teaspoon salt. Set aside ½ cup sauce for gravy and baste turkey with remaining sauce.

When coals are covered with gray ash, spread them out in a line about 2 inches back from the spit and 3 to 4 inches beyond either end of the turkey. Position spit; surface of breast should be about 5 inches from surface of coals. Set a shallow pan made from foil underneath meat to catch drippings.

Cook, adding about 15 briquets every 30 minutes to keep heat level constant; baste often with the sauce. Cook until meat thermometer registers 175° (about 3½ to 4 hours). When turkey is done, move coals as far away as possible. Remove drip pan, drain, and save drippings. Let turkey rest on spit while you make gravy. (If you use a covered barbecue, follow manufacturer's directions.)

Skim most of fat from reserved drippings and discard; measure drippings and add broth made from giblets or chicken broth to make 3½ cups liquid. Gradually blend the ½ cup basting sauce into the flour to make a smooth paste. Add to the 3½ cups liquid in a pan and cook over medium heat, stirring until thickened and boiling. Salt and pepper to taste.

Before serving, remove turkey from spit and place on serving platter. Serve with gravy and onions. Makes 6 to 8 servings with leftover turkey.

## Chile-Barbecued Turkey Drumsticks

Baste turkey with a tangy chile sauce.

1 cup salad oil
½ cup dry red wine
2 tablespoons firmly packed brown sugar
2 teaspoons chile powder
¾ teaspoon each seasoned salt and oregano leaves
¼ teaspoon each garlic powder and seasoned pepper
4 turkey drumsticks (4½ to 5 lbs.)
½ cup sour cream

Combine the salad oil, wine, brown sugar, chile powder, seasoned salt, oregano, garlic powder, and seasoned pepper; shake together in jar or whirl in blender to combine. Pour over turkey drumsticks in a shallow bowl. Cover and chill for about 1 hour, turning once. Drain, reserve marinade, pour marinade into a small pan and heat.

Place drumsticks on grill over slowly burning coals; cover loosely with a tent of heavy foil (or use barbecue cover) and cook, turning and basting occasionally with warm marinade until turkey is tender and well browned (about 2 hours). If you use a covered barbecue, you can expect cooking time to be less (about 1½ hours). Adjust grill height or drafts on barbecue to prevent turkey from browning too quickly. Near end of cooking period, insert a meat thermometer into the thickest part of one of the drumsticks; continue cooking until temperature reaches 185°.

When turkey is nearly done, beat ¼ cup of the remaining marinade gradually into sour cream until blended. Heat sour cream mixture slowly just until heated through (do not boil). Serve sauce separately to spoon over turkey. Makes 4 servings.

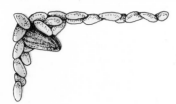
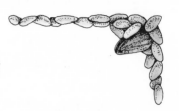

# Try Herbs in Your Next Stuffing

Here's an interesting change from bread cube and poultry seasoning stuffings. One uses rice pilaf and pine nuts, one uses spinach and cheese, the other is made up of shredded apples. You can put the extra stuffing that won't fit in the chicken or turkey in a greased casserole and bake it along with the stuffed bird.

In a large bowl, combine bread, tomato sauce, and eggs; let stand about 15 minutes. Heat the oil in a pan and lightly sauté chicken livers and garlic. Mix soaked bread with your hands until blended. Add livers, oregano, thyme, salt, Parmesan, and spinach; mix well. Makes about 8 cups stuffing.

If you have some left after filling the turkey, put it into a greased casserole and bake, covered, for about 30 minutes.

## Rice Pilaf Stuffing

½ cup pine nuts or slivered almonds
½ cup (¼ lb.) butter or margarine
1 cup finely chopped onion
3 cups long grain rice
½ cup chopped parsley
¼ teaspoon each ground cinnamon and
    ground allspice
2 teaspoons salt
¼ teaspoon pepper
5 cups regular strength chicken broth

Lightly toast the nuts in a 350° oven for 5 to 10 minutes. In a wide frying pan, heat butter and sauté onion about 5 minutes. Add rice and cook, stirring, over medium-high heat for about 4 minutes. Blend in parsley, cinnamon, allspice, salt, pepper, and toasted nuts.

In another pan bring broth to boiling and pour it over rice mixture; stir lightly. Reduce heat to low, cover, and simmer until moisture is absorbed (25 to 30 minutes). Makes about 9 cups stuffing.

## German Apple-Herb Stuffing

1 loaf (15 oz.) firm white bread, cubed
¼ cup each milk and lukewarm water
1 pound lean ground beef, crumbled
    Turkey liver and heart, finely chopped
2 tablespoons butter or margarine
2 cups finely chopped celery
1 large onion, chopped
½ cup chopped parsley
1 large apple, peeled, cored, and shredded
2 eggs, slightly beaten
1 teaspoon each salt and poultry seasoning
⅛ teaspoon pepper

To the bread in a large bowl add milk and water; set aside. Brown ground beef and turkey liver and heart in butter; stir in celery, onion, parsley, and apple. Cook over low heat, stirring occasionally, until celery is soft; cool slightly. Blend lightly with soaked bread, eggs, salt, poultry seasoning, and pepper. Makes about 10 cups stuffing.

## Italian Spinach Stuffing

6 cups cubed sour French bread (about ⅔ loaf,
    in about ½-inch cubes)
1 can (8 oz.) tomato sauce
4 eggs, slightly beaten
¼ cup olive oil or salad oil
½ pound chicken livers, coarsely chopped
4 cloves garlic, minced or mashed
1½ teaspoons oregano leaves
½ teaspoon thyme leaves
1 teaspoon salt
1 cup shredded Parmesan cheese
2 packages (10 or 12 oz. each) frozen chopped
    spinach, thawed and well drained

# Seafood

## *What a Little Basil Can Do for an Oyster...*

## HELPFUL HINTS

Another tasty sauce for shrimp, lobster, or other shell-fish is made by combining 1 small clove garlic (minced) with ½ cup sour cream, ¼ cup canned tomato sauce, 1 tablespoon Cognac (optional), 1 tablespoon anchovy paste, 1 tablespoon lemon juice, a dash of liquid hot pepper seasoning, and 1 teaspoon minced fresh dill or ½ teaspoon dill weed. Chill and serve.

When broiling serving-sized fillets of halibut, lingcod, or rockfish, spread both sides with curry mayonnaise (blend 2 teaspoons curry powder with ⅓ cup mayonnaise), dip in fine dry bread crumbs to coat both sides, then broil.

Spread halibut steaks with Dijon mustard and allow to stand 10 minutes. Dip in slightly beaten egg and fine dry bread crumbs, then sauté in butter. Delicious.

When barbecuing or smoking fish fillets or steaks, lay a branch of fresh herbs such as bay leaf, dill weed, or tarragon leaves on the surface of the fish for additional flavor.

Instead of the usual high-calorie dipping sauces for cracked crab, try an Oriental ginger sauce: To ½ cup rice wine vinegar (or ⅓ cup regular white wine vinegar), add 1 tablespoon water and 1 teaspoon shredded, peeled fresh ginger root, ¼ teaspoon salt, and 2 to 3 tablespoons sweet Sherry or Marin.

# Halibut with Rosemary

Years ago this recipe was devised to preserve fish steaks in Greece. It is called *psari marinata*, or marinated fish. The vinegar and olive oil sauce, aromatic with herbs, permeates the fish steaks to make them delicious hot or cold.

1½ to 2 pounds halibut steaks, swordfish steaks,
    or Greenland turbot fillets
  Salt and pepper
  All-purpose flour
⅓ cup olive oil
¼ cup white wine vinegar
2 tablespoons water
3 cloves garlic
½ teaspoon fresh or dried rosemary leaves

Sprinkle fish steaks with salt and pepper and dust lightly with flour. Heat oil in a large frying pan over medium-high heat; put in fish and cook, turning to brown both sides. Allow about 3 to 4 minutes cooking time per side for swordfish and halibut or 2 minutes for turbot. Test by cutting into center with a sharp knife; when fish becomes opaque white throughout, it is done; then transfer to a hot platter.

Pour vinegar and water into the pan drippings; when it finishes sizzling, add garlic and rosemary and let cook down until reduced by half. Spoon over fish. Makes 4 to 6 servings.

# Baked Halibut and Rice

Halibut and accompanying rice bake together and can be served right from the dish they are cooked in.

¼ cup (⅛ lb.) butter or margarine
1 medium-sized onion, chopped
1 cup each thinly sliced celery and thinly
    sliced carrots
3 cups cooked long grain rice (hot or cold)
¼ cup chopped parsley
½ teaspoon each dill weed and thyme leaves
1 teaspoon salt
1¼ cups milk, scalded
3 eggs
2 to 3 pounds halibut steak or fillet (about ¾
    inch thick)
  Salt and pepper to taste

In a large frying pan, heat 3 tablespoons of the butter over medium heat and sauté the onion, celery, and carrots until almost tender (about 7 minutes). Add the rice, 2 tablespoons of the parsley, dill, thyme, and salt; cook, stirring, until heated through. Spoon into a buttered baking dish

(about 9 by 13 inches). Gradually beat hot milk into eggs, then pour evenly over rice mixture. Sprinkle the fish lightly with salt and pepper and arrange on top of the bed of rice. Melt remaining 1 tablespoon butter and drizzle over the fish.

Bake, uncovered, in a 350° oven until the fish flakes when tested with a fork (about 40 minutes). Sprinkle remaining parsley over top. Makes 6 to 8 servings.

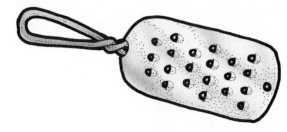

# Baked Sole, Duxelles

Buttery crumbs top sole that bakes on a bed of seasoned mushrooms.

1 tablespoon each olive oil or salad oil and
    all-purpose flour
¼ pound mushrooms, finely chopped
⅓ cup finely chopped shallots or white part of
    green onions
¾ teaspoon tarragon leaves, crushed
½ cup finely chopped parsley
⅓ cup dry white wine or regular strength
    chicken broth
¼ cup whipping cream
1½ to 2 pounds large (1-serving size) sole fillets
  Salt, pepper, and paprika
2 or 3 slices firm white bread
2 tablespoons butter
1 cup shredded Swiss cheese

Put olive oil into a bake-and-serve dish (about 9 by 13 inches); stir in flour and spread mixture over bottom of baking dish. Combine mushrooms with shallots, tarragon, and ¼ cup of the parsley; sprinkle evenly over bottom of baking dish. Drizzle with the wine and cream.

Sprinkle fillets lightly with salt, pepper, and paprika and arrange attractively on top of vegetables so they overlap only slightly. Whirl bread in blender (or pull apart with fork) to make 1 cup fresh crumbs. Melt butter in a pan and stir crumbs over medium heat until lightly toasted; set aside. (This can be done ahead; cover and refrigerate the fish.)

Before serving, mix remaining ¼ cup parsley with buttered crumbs and sprinkle over fish. Bake, uncovered, in a 350° oven for about 20 minutes (about 40 minutes if refrigerated) or until fish flakes when tested with a fork. Sprinkle cheese over top and return to oven just until cheese melts. Makes 6 servings.

## Broiled Salmon with Mustard Sauce

When broiling thick salmon steaks, liberally spread them with a creamy mustard-flavored sauce just before they are done.

1 cup sour cream
½ cup finely chopped green onion
1½ tablespoons Dijon mustard
1 tablespoon chopped parsley
½ teaspoon each *salt, thyme, and marjoram leaves*
Dash pepper
4 salmon steaks, each *cut 1 inch thick*
Salt and pepper

Stir together the sour cream, green onion, mustard, parsley, salt, thyme, marjoram, and pepper; set aside.

Sprinkle salmon steaks lightly with salt and pepper. To broil, line a shallow pan with foil, arrange steaks on the foil, and broil about 6 inches below a preheated broiler for 7 minutes. Remove pan from oven, turn steaks over, and spread the top of each steak generously with the cream sauce. Return to broiler and broil about 5 minutes longer or until fish flakes with a fork. Makes 4 servings.

## Poached Salmon with Horseradish Butter

Wine-poached center cut of salmon is enhanced by a horseradish-flavored butter sauce and paprika-dusted lemon halves.

1 pint (2 cups) water
1 cup dry white wine
1 each *carrot, onion, celery stalk*
1 teaspoon salt
1 bay leaf
6 whole black peppers
½ teaspoon thyme leaves
2 to 2½-pound center cut piece salmon
½ cup (¼ lb.) sweet (unsalted) butter
2 tablespoons prepared horseradish
  Parsley
2 lemons
  Paprika

Place in a large saucepan the water, wine, peeled carrot, peeled onion, trimmed celery, salt, bay leaf, peppers, and thyme. Bring to a boil, reduce heat, and simmer 15 minutes.

Wrap salmon loosely in cheesecloth to facilitate removing it from pan, slip into poaching liquid, and barely simmer about 12 to 15 minutes or until fish flakes when tested with a fork. With a spatula, lift out to a hot serving dish and remove cheesecloth; keep warm. Strain poaching liquid and reserve ¼ cup for sauce.

For sauce, heat butter until melted; stir in horseradish and ¼ cup juice strained from the poaching liquid. Pour into a small serving pitcher. Garnish fish platter with parsley and lemon halves dusted with paprika. Cut salmon into serving-size pieces, removing skin; pour the melted, seasoned butter over fish. Makes 6 to 8 servings.

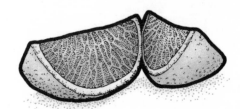

## Poached Turbot with Guacamole

Turbot and guacamole are a delicious combination of textures and flavors. Serve chilled or hot.

2 cups water
1 small onion, sliced
3 whole black peppers
1 whole allspice
2 tablespoons lime juice or lemon juice
1 teaspoon salt
1½ to 2 pounds Greenland turbot fillets, completely thawed
  Guacamole Sauce (recipe follows)
  Lime slices for garnish (optional)

In a wide frying pan, combine the water, onion, peppers, allspice, lime juice, and salt. Bring to boiling and simmer for about 10 minutes. Cut fish into serving-sized pieces and set into pan. Cover and simmer gently until fish flakes when tested with a fork (about 6 minutes). With a wide spatula, carefully remove fish from liquid and arrange on serving plate.

Serve hot with Guacamole Sauce; garnish the hot fish with thin slices of lime. Or cover the plate and chill fish and guacamole separately. Spread guacamole over top of chilled fish. Makes 6 servings.

*Guacamole Sauce.* Combine 1 can (7¾ oz.) frozen avocado dip, thawed, with ¼ cup sour cream, 2 green onions thinly sliced, 1 tablespoon finely chopped parsley, 1 tablespoon lime or lemon juice, ½ teaspoon salt, ⅛ teaspoon liquid hot pepper seasoning, and ½ teaspoon ground coriander (optional); stir until blended.

## Dungeness Crab and Greenland Turbot Stew

Both have similar flavor and texture and go together naturally in this stew. When crab is out of season, you can make it entirely of turbot, using about 3 pounds; serve with sour cream.

2 large onions, finely chopped
2 tablespoons olive oil or salad oil
¾ cup catsup
2¼ cups regular strength chicken broth
1-inch piece cinnamon stick
½ teaspoon thyme leaves
1 tablespoon Worcestershire
3 or 4 thin lemon slices
2 pounds Greenland turbot fillets (thawed if frozen), cut in about 1½-inch chunks
1 large (about 2 lbs.) cooked Dungeness crab, cleaned and cracked
Lemon wedges
Salt

In a kettle (at least 4-qt. size) cook onion in oil until soft, stirring. Add catsup, broth, cinnamon, thyme, Worcestershire, and lemon slices and bring to a boil. Cover and simmer for 15 minutes. Remove cinnamon and lemon slices and discard. Place turbot chunks in sauce, then lay crab on top. Bring to a simmer; cover pan and cook 10 to 15 minutes or until turbot pieces flake readily when prodded. Ladle into wide, deep bowls; squeeze the lemon wedges over the stew and add salt to taste. Makes 5 to 6 servings.

## Baked Fish with Piquant Sauce

Use thick fillets or steaks of sturgeon, sea bass, or halibut for this Portuguese-style baked fish dish.

2 to 3 pounds thick (about 1 inch) fish steaks or fillets
1 teaspoon salt
About 2 tablespoons all-purpose flour
2 medium sized onions, sliced
¼ cup olive oil
⅓ cup white wine vinegar
3 cloves garlic, minced or mashed
1 teaspoon each oregano leaves and prepared mustard
⅛ teaspoon powdered saffron (optional)
1 tablespoon each fresh minced parsley and coriander (or use 2 tablespoons dried parsley and ¼ teaspoon ground coriander)
1 tablespoon lemon juice
About ¼ cup water or dry white wine
Lemon wedges (optional)

Sprinkle fish with salt, then dust lightly all over with flour. Arrange fish in a shallow baking dish (about 8 by 12 inches). In a frying pan, sauté the onions in oil until limp, then distribute over fish. Combine wine vinegar, garlic, oregano, mustard, saffron (if used), parsley, coriander, and lemon juice; mix well and pour over fish. Pour water around fish. Bake, uncovered, in a 350° oven until the fish flakes easily when tested with a fork (about 45 minutes); add a little water if liquid cooks away. Serve with lemon if you wish. Makes about 6 servings.

## Paella

This adaptation of paella (pronounced pay-ay-yah) can simmer relatively unattended on the top of the range in a deep kettle, or you can bake it in the oven. It can be partly prepared the day before.

2 pounds chicken legs and thighs, separated
2 tablespoons olive oil or salad oil
3 medium-sized (about 8 oz.) mildly seasoned chorizos, crumbled
4 slices bacon, diced
1 large onion, chopped
2 cloves garlic, minced or mashed
1¼ cups long grain rice
⅛ teaspoon powdered saffron (optional)
1 can (about 1 lb.) stewed tomatoes
1 can (about 14 oz.) regular strength chicken broth
2 tablespoons each minced parsley and white wine vinegar
½ cup dry white wine
1 teaspoon each oregano leaves, ground coriander, paprika, and salt
1 pound medium-sized shrimp, shelled and deveined
1 package (10 oz.) frozen peas, thawed
2 cans (about 3½ oz. each) smoked clams or smoked oysters, well drained

In a large kettle (at least 5-quart capacity), brown chicken pieces well in the olive oil over medium-high heat. Remove chicken and set aside; discard any fat in the pan. Add chorizos and bacon to pan and cook, stirring until lightly browned. Add the onion and garlic and cook, stirring, until soft.

Add the rice and the saffron (if used) to pan and stir until rice is lightly browned (about 5 minutes). Add the tomatoes, chicken broth, parsley, vinegar, wine, oregano, coriander, paprika, and salt to the pan. Arrange chicken pieces on top. Cover. (Refrigerate for up to one day if made ahead.) Bring mixture to boiling over medium heat, stirring as necessary, then simmer until chicken and rice are tender (about 20 minutes). Add the shrimp, cover, and simmer for 5 minutes or until shrimp are firm and pink. Remove pan from heat.

With tongs remove chicken pieces and set aside; keep warm. Stir peas and smoked clams into rice mixture. If desired, transfer mixture to a wide deep serving platter. Arrange chicken around rice mixture. Makes 10 to 12 servings.

*Baked Paella.* Follow recipe above but with these changes: transfer browned, uncooked rice mixture to a 5-quart casserole or roasting pan and top with the browned chicken. Cover pan tightly, then bake in a 350° oven for 45 minutes (1 hour if refrigerated). Add the shrimp, replace cover, and bake for 15 minutes more. Add the peas and clams or oysters and serve as directed above.

## Crabe à l'Américaine

A faint hint of curry, white wine, and brandy blends with delicately flavored crab in this hot dish topped with toasted buttered crumbs.

*2 tablespoons butter or margarine*
*1 medium-sized onion, finely chopped*
*¼ pound mushrooms, thinly sliced*
*½ teaspoon curry powder*
*3 tablespoons tomato paste*
*1 tablespoon brandy*
*¼ cup dry white wine*
*½ cup whipping cream*
*1 pound fresh shelled crab*
*  Salt and pepper*
*  Buttered Crumbs (directions follow)*
*  Chopped parsley*

Melt butter in a wide frying pan over medium heat and add the onion and mushrooms; cook, stirring, until vegetables are limp. Stir in curry powder, tomato paste, brandy, wine, and cream; bring mixture to a boil and remove from heat. Gently blend crab meat into the vegetables. Salt and pepper to taste.

Evenly divide the crab among 6 ovenproof, individual serving dishes or scallop shells. Top each dish with an even layer of buttered crumbs. (At this point you can cover and chill crab up to 8 hours, if you wish.) Bake, uncovered, in a 400° oven for about 10 minutes or until crumbs are lightly toasted and crab is just hot. (Bake about 10 to 15 minutes if refrigerated.) Lightly sprinkle chopped parsley over each dish. Serve at once. Makes 6 first course servings.

*Buttered Crumbs.* Whirl in a blender until coarsely ground, enough white bread (about 2 slices) to make 1 cup of crumbs. In a small bowl, mix the crumbs with 2 tablespoons melted butter.

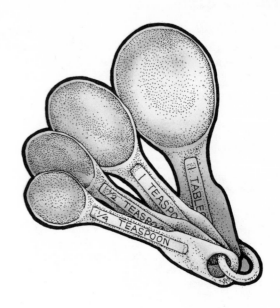

## Cracked Crab in Spicy Red Sauce

Ask your fish dealer to clean and crack freshly cooked crabs. Before serving, prepare the sauce. Then simply add pieces of crab to sauce and heat.

*¼ cup (⅛ lb.) butter or margarine*
*2 large onions, finely chopped*
*2 cloves garlic, minced or mashed*
*1 large can (15 oz.) tomato sauce*
*½ cup catsup*
*1 large can (about 47 oz.) regular strength*
*  chicken broth*
*¾ teaspoon marjoram leaves, crushed*
*1 teaspoon basil leaves, crushed*
*2 tablespoons each Worcestershire and prepared*
*  horseradish*
*¼ cup chopped parsley*
*1 bay leaf*
*2 large cooked Dungeness crabs (about 2 lbs.*
*  each) cleaned and cracked*
*  Lemon wedges*

In a large kettle (at least 5-qt. size), melt the butter over medium heat; add onion and garlic and cook until onion is limp (about 5 minutes). Stir in tomato sauce, catsup, broth, marjoram, basil, Worcestershire, horseradish, parsley, and bay. Bring to a boil, reduce heat, and simmer, uncovered, for 10 to 15 minutes, stirring occasionally until slightly thickened. Add crab, cover, and simmer 10 more minutes or until crab is heated through. Remove bay leaf and ladle crab and sauce into bowls. Pass lemon to squeeze over individual servings. Makes about 4 servings.

## Sautéed Oysters with Basil

Oysters benefit from light cooking. These you brown briefly in butter, then flavor with wine.

8 *Eastern or 6 medium-sized Pacific oysters*
   *(usually sold in jars)*
   *All-purpose flour*
2 *tablespoons butter*
½ *teaspoon basil leaves, crushed*
2 *tablespoons dry white wine*

Gently pat dry the oysters. If in shells, cut free and remove. Dredge in flour, then dust off excess. Place a 10-inch frying pan over highest heat. Melt the butter, add oysters, and sprinkle the basil over them. Brown oysters lightly for about 2 minutes for each side. Arrange each in a half shell or divide between two individual serving dishes; keep warm. To the pan add the wine; quickly stir to release browned particles, then spoon liquid over oysters. Makes 2 first course servings.

# Making Herb Bouquets at Home

An herb bouquet (*bouquet garni* in French) combines herbs to flavor foods. The two below are made by tying fresh herbs together by the stems or carefully tying dried herbs in small cheesecloth bags for use. Add them while the dish cooks. Remove them just before serving the dish.

Fresh herb bouquets can be packed in small plastic bags or wrapped well in clear film or foil and frozen. If you make either the fresh or dried bouquets ahead, be sure to label them for the specific dishes they are intended.

### Basic mixture for fresh herb bouquet

Tie together 3 or 4 sprigs parsley, 1 bay leaf, and 2 sprigs thyme with a coarse white cotton thread or fine cotton twine.

*Variations:* For seafood, add 4 or 5 chives to each bouquet. For poultry, add a sprig of marjoram to each bouquet. For tomato dishes, add a sprig of basil. For beef or lamb, add a small sprig of rosemary.

### Basic mixture for dried herb bouquet

Mix together ½ cup dried parsley flakes, and ¼ cup thyme leaves. For each dried bouquet you make, place 1 teaspoon of this mixture on a 3-inch square of cheesecloth (double thickness) along with ¼ bay leaf. Gather up the sides of the cheesecloth and tie, leaving a 6-inch length of thread for easy handling.

*Variations:* For seafood, add 2 tablespoons dried lemon peel and 2 whole black peppers to the basic mixture. For brown stock, add 1 whole clove, 2 whole black peppers, and a small piece of dried mace to each bouquet. For tomato soups and sauce, add 1 tablespoon oregano leaves, 2 tablespoons dried basil leaves, 1 whole clove, and 2 whole black peppers.

# Vegetables

## *Standards Become Special When You Add an Herb or Two*

## HELPFUL HINTS

Liven up tomatoes by slicing them in half, crosswise, then dotting the cut surfaces with butter. Sprinkle lightly with dry mustard, salt, and pepper. Broil until heated through.

Cool pleasures come by way of thinly sliced cucumbers, peeled and gently mixed with ¼ cup sour cream (or yogurt) and ½ teaspoon garlic salt and minced fresh mint (or ½ teaspoon crushed dried mint). Chill before serving.

Add new zip to beets. Beat together ¼ cup butter, 1 tablespoon *each* prepared mustard and tarragon vinegar. Mix mustard butter into about 3 cups hot, cooked diced beets to season.

Sprinkle a few anise seeds on your carrots when they are cooking for an herby blending of flavors.

Season freshly cooked peas with lemon mint butter. Cream together ½ cup butter, 1 tablespoon lemon juice, ¼ teaspoon grated lemon peel, and 2 to 3 tablespoons finely chopped fresh mint. Melt flavored butter over peas.

Sauté thin slices of red bell peppers in 3 tablespoons salad oil, 2 tablespoons water, and ½ teaspoon whole cumin seed. Cook over medium heat, stirring, until peppers are limp and liquid has evaporated. Salt to taste. Makes a bright red accompaniment for any dish.

## Glazed Paprika Onions

Very easy to prepare, this dish cooks in the oven while you prepare the rest of the meal.

4 large mild red onions (about 2 lbs.)
¼ teaspoon rubbed sage
½ teaspoon each dry mustard and salt
¾ teaspoon paprika
2 tablespoons red wine vinegar
5 teaspoons honey
¼ cup melted butter or margarine

Peel and slice the onions in half crosswise. Place them, cut side up, side by side so they fit closely in a shallow baking pan.

Mix together in a small bowl the sage, dry mustard, salt, paprika, vinegar, and honey. Pour this mixture evenly over the onion halves. Cover the pan tightly and bake in a 350° oven for about 1 hour or until onions are tender when pierced.

Baste several times, using the sauce in the pan. Remove the cover and drizzle the butter evenly over the onion halves. Continue baking for about 10 minutes or until onions are glazed and most of the liquid has evaporated. Pour any remaining sauce over onions. Makes 8 servings.

## Indian Eggplant Slices

This brilliantly colored eggplant dish mingles two sauces—hot gingered tomato and chilled yogurt or sour cream.

1 medium-sized onion, finely chopped
2 tablespoons butter or margarine
1 can (about 14 oz.) pear shaped tomatoes
1 tablespoon sugar
1 teaspoon finely chopped fresh ginger root
    or ¼ teaspoon ground ginger
¼ teaspoon salt
    Dash of freshly ground pepper
1 large eggplant (about 1 lb.)
½ cup olive oil or salad oil
½ pint (1 cup) unflavored yogurt or sour cream
    (or ½ cup of each)
2 tablespoons finely chopped parsley

Using a large saucepan, sauté onion in butter until golden brown. Whirl tomatoes and their liquid in a blender until smooth (or press through a wire strainer); add to onion mixture along with sugar, ginger, salt, and pepper. Simmer, uncovered, until thick (about 10 minutes).

Meanwhile, slice unpeeled eggplant ¾ inch thick and pour oil into a baking pan (about 10 by 15 inches). Dip eggplant slices in oil, coating both sides, then arrange in a single layer in the pan; bake in a 450° oven for 30 minutes or until tender, turning once.

Arrange eggplant in a single layer on a serving dish, spoon a coating of yogurt over each, and top with tomato sauce, leaving a narrow border of yogurt. Sprinkle with parsley. Makes 6 servings.

## Leeks with Tarragon

Trimming is the secret to cleaning leeks. Trim the tops by making a diagonal cut from each side to the center point so that only about 1½ inches of the dark green leaves remain. Split leeks in half lengthwise to within ⅓-inch of bulb end or split large stalks completely through. Strip away the outer 2 or 3 layers of leaves until you reach the non-fibrous interior leaves. Hold leeks under running water and gently separate layers to wash.

2 pounds (about 6) leeks
4 cups salted water
2 tablespoons butter or margarine
1 tablespoon chopped parsley
1 teaspoon finely chopped fresh tarragon
    (or ¼ teaspoon dried tarragon leaves)
¼ cup grated Parmesan cheese

*(Continued on next page)*

Trim and clean leeks, following directions above. In a large frying pan with a cover, bring water to boil; add leeks and simmer, covered, until tender (about 10 to 15 minutes, depending on sizes). Lift leeks from water as each is cooked tender; drain and arrange in a serving dish and keep warm. Melt butter and stir in parsley, tarragon, and cheese. Pour over leeks and serve. Makes 4 to 6 servings.

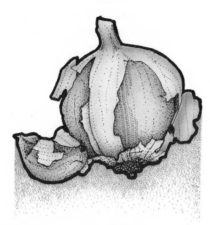

## Garlic Creamed Spinach

A robust Italian touch gives this simple spinach dish an unexpected character with a well-defined flavor of sautéed garlic.

1½ *pounds fresh spinach or 2 packages (10 oz.*
    *each) frozen leaf or chopped spinach*
  *1 tablespoon each olive oil and butter or*
    *margarine*
  *1 large onion, finely chopped*
  *4 cloves garlic*
  *2 tablespoons all-purpose flour*
  *¾ cup half-and-half (light cream) or sour*
    *cream*
  *¼ teaspoon ground nutmeg*
  *1 cup freshly grated Parmesan cheese*
    *Salt and pepper to taste*

If you use fresh spinach, place washed, damp spinach leaves in a large pan, cover, and place on medium heat. Stir occasionally until leaves are wilted (takes 3 to 4 minutes). If using frozen, follow package directions. You should have 2 to 2½ cups chopped cooked spinach.

Combine the oil and butter in a wide frying pan over medium-high heat. When butter is melted, add the onion and garlic; cook, stirring, until onion is soft. Stir in the flour, blending well. Remove from heat and blend in the half-and-half (or sour cream) and nutmeg. Add the spinach and return to high heat, stirring, until bubbling vigorously.

Remove from heat and mix in ½ cup of the cheese and the salt and pepper. Serve hot, sprinkled with the remaining ½ cup cheese.

(To make this dish ahead, spoon cooked spinach mixture into a shallow, 3 to 4-cup casserole, sprinkle with the ½ cup cheese; cover, and chill. Bake, uncovered, in a 375° oven for 12 to 15 minutes or until hot through. Serve topped with remaining cheese.) Makes 4 to 5 servings.

## Indian Mixed Vegetables

Turmeric gives this dish its golden color. You might serve it with a curry dinner or with a lamb roast or chicken.

  *¼ cup (⅛ lb.) butter*
  *1 medium-sized onion, sliced*
  *¼ teaspoon ground turmeric*
  *½ teaspoon summer savory*
  *1 large potato, peeled and cubed*
1½ *cups water*
  *1 small head cabbage, shredded*
  *1 small cauliflower, cut in small pieces*
  *1 cup fresh or frozen peas*
  *2 fresh tomatoes, peeled and cut into wedges*
  *1 bunch spinach, washed, with stems removed*
    *About 2 teaspoons salt*

In a large pan (about 5-quart size), melt the butter; add the onion, turmeric, and savory. Sauté until the onion is limp (about 5 minutes). Add the potato and water; cover and cook about 5 minutes. Add the cabbage and cauliflower and simmer about 5 minutes, then add the peas, tomatoes, and spinach; cook about 3 to 5 minutes. Add salt to taste and stir gently. Transfer to serving bowl immediately and keep warm on the buffet table. Makes 12 servings.

## Basque Stewed Potatoes with Parsley

Parsley, stirred into potatoes previously simmered tender in broth, adds a freshness that makes this dish particularly tasty.

  *1 medium-sized onion, thinly sliced*
  *1 whole clove garlic*
  *3 tablespoons olive oil*
  *2 pounds (about 4 medium) baking potatoes*
    *cut in ¼-inch thick slices*
1¼ *cups regular strength chicken or beef broth*
  *½ cup minced parsley*
    *Salt*

In a 2-quart saucepan cook the onion and garlic, stirring, in the olive oil until onion is soft but not browned.

Add the potatoes to the onions and pour in the chicken or beef broth; cover and simmer for about 25 minutes or until potatoes are easily pierced with a fork. Stir gently, occasionally. Blend in the parsley and cook about 1 minute longer, then season with salt to taste and serve at once. Makes 6 to 8 servings.

## Danish Sweet and Sour Cabbage

If you cook red cabbage in salted water like other vegetables, its color changes to an unappetizing shade of blue. It needs to have something tart added to it, such as apples or vinegar, to develop the familiar rich wine color we recognize in cooked red cabbage.

1 medium sized (about 2 lbs.) red cabbage
4 tablespoons (⅛ lb.) butter or margarine
½ cup water
3 tablespoons each cider vinegar and red currant jelly
½ teaspoon caraway seed (optional)
Salt to taste

Finely shred the cabbage. In a 3 or 4-quart saucepan over medium-high heat, melt the butter; stir in the cabbage, water, vinegar, jelly, and caraway seed, if you wish.

Bring to a boil, cover, and simmer gently for 1½ hours, stirring occasionally; add a little more water if cabbage cooks dry. Salt to taste and serve hot. Makes 6 servings.

## Marinated Green Beans, Carrots, or Cauliflower

You can use these vegetables immediately or within two weeks.

2 pounds green beans, carrots, or cauliflower
2 quarts water
3 tablespoons coarse (Kosher-style) salt
2 teaspoons each mustard seed and dill weed
1 teaspoon crushed small dried hot chile peppers
1 teaspoon dill seed
4 cloves garlic
2 cups water
2 cups white vinegar
⅔ cup sugar

Snip ends from beans and wash thoroughly; leave whole or cut in half if long. Peel carrots and cut into thin sticks. Separate cauliflower into flowerets. In a large pan, bring the 2 quarts water to boil; add 1 tablespoon of the salt and the beans, carrots, or cauliflower. Let water return to a boil and cook, uncovered, for about 5 minutes for beans and 3 minutes for carrots or cauliflower (or just until vegetables are tender-crisp). Drain immediately and cool. Pack into 4 refrigerator containers (1-pint size). Into each container put ½ teaspoon each mustard seed and dill weed, ¼ teaspoon each chiles and dill seed, and 1 clove garlic.

Bring to a boil the 2 cups each water and vinegar, the ⅔ cup sugar, and remaining 2 tablespoons salt; pour over vegetables. Cool, cover; refrigerate for as long as 2 weeks. Makes 4 pints.

## Mint Hollandaise with Vegetables

Pass the Mint Hollandaise to spoon over lightly cooked vegetables. Cook small whole carrots, broccoli spears, or fresh green beans in a small amount of boiling water. Drain and arrange on a large serving platter.

⅔ cup melted butter or margarine
3 egg yolks
1 tablespoon white wine vinegar
1 teaspoon sugar
Dash salt
½ cup finely chopped fresh mint leaves
⅓ cup whipping cream, whipped stiff

Heat the butter until melted and bubbly. In a blender container, whirl egg yolks, vinegar, sugar, salt, and mint until well blended; then, with the motor running, very gradually pour the hot butter in a slow, steady stream. Blend just until the melted butter is incorporated into the sauce. Cool, cover, and chill until thick; fold into whipped cream. Cover and chill until needed. Makes 1½ cups.

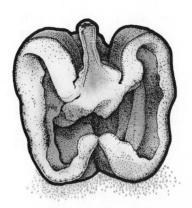

## Cinnamon Carrot Sticks

Carrots readily absorb flavors, yet retain their appealing crispness when they are briefly cooked and then chilled in a spicy bath.

12 large carrots (2 to 2½ lbs.)
2½ cups water
½ cup cider vinegar
¾ cup sugar
1 stick cinnamon

Peel and cut carrots into sticks about ½ by 3 inches. Place in a large pan with the water and boil, covered, until just tender when pierced (7 to 10 minutes). Drain, saving liquid. Turn carrots into a bowl. To carrot liquid add the vinegar, sugar, cinnamon; bring to a boil and pour over carrots. Cool, cover, and chill overnight or as long as 2 to 3 weeks. Makes about 7 cups.

## Smoke-Barbecued Pinto Beans

If you are serving a large group, this recipe may just suit your purpose. It will serve a dozen or more.

2 pounds dried pinto beans
About 2½ quarts water
1 pound slab bacon without rind, or thick-sliced bacon
3 medium-sized onions, sliced
2 cans (about 14 oz. each) pear shaped tomatoes
About 2 teaspoons salt
About ½ teaspoon pepper
2 tablespoons chile powder
1 teaspoon oregano leaves
2 tablespoons dry mustard
⅛ teaspoon cumin seed
3 tablespoons water
1 cup dark molasses
Salt and pepper to taste

Wash beans thoroughly and place in large kettle with 2½ quarts water. Soak overnight. The next day, add water, if necessary, to cover beans and bring them to a boil.

Meanwhile, cut bacon slab into ¾-inch cubes and add to beans, together with onions and tomatoes. Cover and simmer until beans are tender (about 2 hours).

Mix 2 teaspoons salt, ½ teaspoon pepper, chile powder, oregano, mustard, and cumin, and slowly add the 3 tablespoons water to spices to make a thin paste. Stir this into the beans with the molasses; pour mixture into a large deep roasting pan or other pan that holds at least 6 quarts.

If you have a smoker or smoke oven, follow manufacturer's directions for smoking. Place the beans, uncovered, in the smoker and cook at about 300° for about 2 hours.

If you use a covered barbecue, arrange a small number of glowing coals about 6 inches beneath the grill on each side or in a circle around where the beans will sit. Sprinkle charcoal with hickory chips and place beans, uncovered, in the center of the grill.

Cover barbecue, adjust the temperature control dampers to maintain low glowing coals, and smoke-cook for about 2 hours. Add some more charcoal and hickory chips as needed to produce a generous amount of smoke; stir beans about every 30 minutes.

Or place the beans, uncovered, in a 300° oven for 2 hours. Season to taste with salt and pepper. Makes about 4 quarts beans.

## Broccoli with Lemon Cream

Use a deep, heatproof serving plate or an oval baking dish for this.

2 pounds fresh broccoli
Boiling salted water
2 packages (3 oz. each) cream cheese, at room temperature
6 tablespoons milk
1 teaspoon grated lemon peel
1 tablespoon lemon juice
½ teaspoon each ground ginger and cardamom
½ cup sliced or slivered almonds
1 tablespoon butter

Trim and peel stem ends of fresh broccoli spears; cook in boiling water just until tender-crisp (about 7 minutes). Drain and arrange neatly, with spears all pointing in same direction, in a heat-proof serving dish. Combine the cream cheese with milk, lemon peel and juice, ginger, and cardamom; beat until smoothly blended. Spoon the cheese mixture over broccoli stems, leaving some of the green heads showing. (This much can be done ahead; then cover and refrigerate.)

To serve, cover with the casserole lid or with foil and bake in a 350° oven for about 15 minutes (25 minutes if refrigerated) or until heated through. Sauté almonds in the butter in a small pan until toasted. Sprinkle over top of vegetables before serving. Makes 6 to 8 servings.

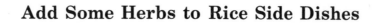

# Add Some Herbs to Rice Side Dishes

A rice dish that is seasoned to complement the entrée is an easy way to add distinction to the menu.

## Brazilian Rice

Serve this spicy brown rice dish with any simply seasoned roast of beef or with chicken or turkey.

To 3 cups boiling water in a saucepan, add 2 cups quick-cooking brown rice, 3 tablespoons butter, $\frac{1}{8}$ teaspoon garlic powder, and 1 teaspoon *each* brown sugar, salt, chile powder, and grated orange peel. Stir, cover, reduce heat, and cook for 20 minutes. Remove from heat and add 1 cup sliced Brazil nuts or almonds and 1 can ($2\frac{1}{2}$ oz.) sliced black olives. Makes 8 servings.

## Golden Rice

Lamb, fish, or egg entrées are nicely complemented by this turmeric flavored rice.

Bring to a boil in a large saucepan 5 cups water, $\frac{1}{4}$ teaspoon ground turmeric, 2 teaspoons salt, and 2 tablespoons butter. Stir in 2 cups long grain white rice. Cover and simmer 25 minutes (or until tender). Add $\frac{1}{2}$ cup golden raisins. Heat $\frac{1}{2}$ cup butter until bubbly and slightly brown; pour over rice. Stir lightly with a fork to distribute melted butter and raisins evenly. Makes 8 servings.

## Cumin Rice with Pine Nuts

Serve with chicken, turkey, beef, lamb, or pork. Melt $1\frac{1}{2}$ tablespoons butter in a pan, add $1\frac{1}{2}$ cups long grain rice and stir until it turns golden brown. Add $1\frac{1}{2}$ teaspoons salt, 1 tablespoon ground cumin, and 4 cups boiling water. Cover and simmer about 25 minutes or until rice is fluffy and dry. Spoon into a serving dish; keep warm. Melt 3 more tablespoons butter and add $\frac{1}{2}$ cup pine nuts or slivered almonds; sauté, shaking the pan until nuts are golden brown. Spoon over hot rice. Makes 6 to 8 servings.

## Green Rice

This rice and spinach combination flatters most meat, fish, and poultry entrées.

Cook 1 cup long grain rice as the package directs. Remove from heat and add $\frac{1}{4}$ cup ($\frac{1}{8}$ lb.) butter, 2 teaspoons lemon juice, $\frac{1}{2}$ cup slivered or sliced almonds, 1 clove garlic (minced), 1 medium-sized onion (chopped), 2 cups firmly packed, finely chopped spinach, $\frac{1}{2}$ cup *each* chopped green onion tops and finely chopped parsley, $\frac{1}{2}$ teaspoon salt, and $\frac{1}{4}$ teaspoon *each* crumbled marjoram and basil leaves. Beat 1 egg with 1 cup milk and stir into rice. Mix lightly, then turn into a greased, $2\frac{1}{2}$-quart baking dish. Bake, uncovered, in a 350° oven for 30 minutes (cook for 1 hour if cold) or until custard is set; mix lightly. Makes 4 to 6 servings.

## Ginger Coconut Rice

This rice will team up nicely with lamb or other meat curry. The coconut lends a slightly sweet flavor to it. Melt $\frac{1}{2}$ cup ($\frac{1}{4}$ lb.) butter in a large, heavy pan. Add 2 medium-sized onions (thinly sliced) and 2 teaspoons finely grated fresh ginger root (or 1 teaspoon ground ginger); sauté until the onion is limp but not browned. Add 3 cups long grain rice and continue cooking slowly until the rice turns opaque. Stir in $4\frac{1}{2}$ cups regular strength chicken broth, cover, and reduce heat. Simmer slowly for 10 minutes. Stir in $\frac{3}{4}$ cup fresh or packaged grated coconut and continue cooking for about 15 minutes or until rice is tender and the liquid absorbed. Makes 12 servings.

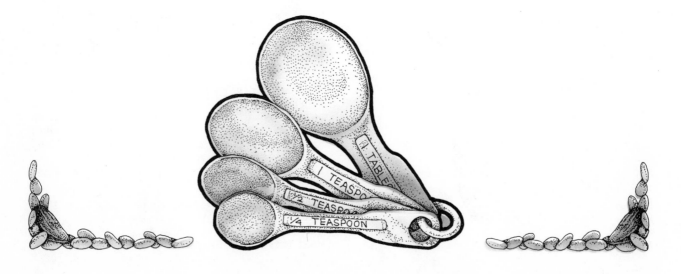

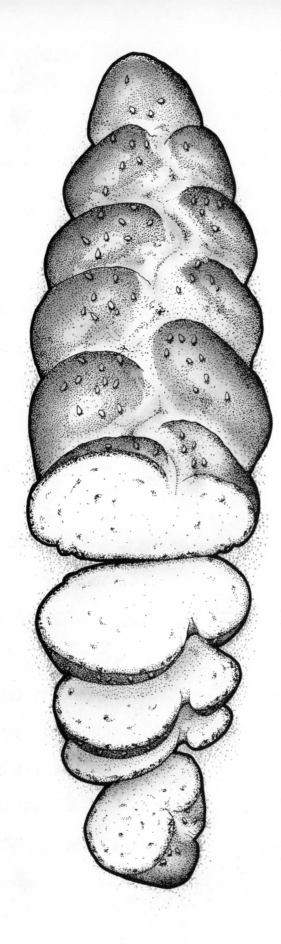

# Breads

## Quick Breads, Yeast Breads, Muffins, Coffee Cake

### HELPFUL HINTS

When making white bread why not add an herb to the dough, using the following amounts for each loaf: 1 tablespoon savory leaves; $1\frac{1}{2}$ teaspoons basil leaves; $1\frac{1}{2}$ teaspoons oregano leaves; $1\frac{1}{2}$ teaspoons thyme leaves; or $2\frac{1}{4}$ teaspoons marjoram leaves.

For cinnamon waffles, use a pancake and waffle mix or biscuit mix, preparing according to directions on package. Add $\frac{1}{2}$ teaspoon ground cinnamon for each cup of dry mix, then bake as usual.

Serve a simple cardamom bread made of flour tortillas in a stack. Blend $\frac{1}{4}$ cup soft butter with $\frac{1}{4}$ teaspoon ground cardamom. Spread lightly on 8 flour tortillas; stack tortillas and wrap in foil; heat in a 300° oven for 20 minutes. Guests roll up their own tortillas and eat.

A change from garlic bread: spread French bread slices with onion-seed butter. For each cup of softened butter blend in 1 cup finely minced green onion and $\frac{1}{4}$ cup sesame seed or poppy seed. Or spread sourdough French bread slices with a mixture of $\frac{1}{4}$ pound butter, $\frac{1}{2}$ cup each very finely minced parsley and chopped pecans, 1 small clove garlic (puréed), and a pinch of salt. Serve warmed or unheated.

For bite and flavor, try pepper rolls. Use a hot roll mix and add 2 teaspoons freshly crushed black pepper to the dough; mix and bake according to package directions. Serve hot with butter.

## Sesame Wheat Germ Cornbread

Toasted sesame seeds give a nutty flavor and crunchiness to this cornbread.

   1½ cups all-purpose flour, unsifted
   ½ cup sugar
   1½ teaspoons salt
   1¼ teaspoons soda
   2 cups cornmeal
   1 cup wheat germ
   ½ cup (2¾ oz.) sesame seed, toasted
   2 cups buttermilk
   ¾ cup salad oil or melted butter
   2 eggs, slightly beaten

Sift together the flour, sugar, salt, and soda; blend in the cornmeal, wheat germ, and sesame seed. In a separate bowl, mix together the buttermilk, salad oil or melted butter, and eggs. Blend the dry ingredients and the liquid mixture together, using a minimum number of strokes. Pour into a greased loaf pan (9 by 5 inches) and bake in a 375° oven for about 55 minutes. Remove bread from pan and cool on a rack. Makes 1 large loaf.

## Oat Sesame Bread

Toasted sesame seed accents the flavor of this bread made with rolled oats.

   1 cup regular rolled oats
   2 cups boiling water
   ½ cup sesame seed
   1 package active dry or compressed yeast
   ½ cup warm (about 105°) water (lukewarm for
      compressed yeast)
   ¼ cup each dark molasses and dark corn
      syrup
   1½ teaspoons salt
   3 tablespoons melted butter or margarine
      About 4½ cups all-purpose flour, unsifted

Stir together oats and boiling water in the top of a double boiler; cover and cook over simmering water until water in the top pan is absorbed (about 1 hour). Transfer oats to a large bowl; let cool. In a frying pan over medium heat, stir sesame seed until browned.

Dissolve yeast in the ½ cup water, then add to cooled oats. Stir in molasses, corn syrup, salt, 2 tablespoons of the butter, and sesame seed. Gradually stir in 4 cups flour. Spread remaining ½ cup flour on a board. Turn dough out and knead well, lifting the edge of the dough farthest away from you, folding in half toward you, then, with your palms, pressing dough down and away. Turn dough a quarter turn and repeat, lifting, folding,

and pressing. Continue without turning dough over until it is elastic and non-sticky; sprinkle additional flour on the board and on your hands as needed to prevent sticking. The dough will be sufficiently kneaded when it looks smooth, has a slight sheen, and feels velvety and resilient. (Total time: about 10 minutes.) Let dough rise, covered, in a greased bowl until almost doubled (about 2 hours).

Punch down dough and squeeze it to release air bubbles, then divide into two equal portions. Knead lightly and gently on a very lightly floured board just until the portion of dough has a smooth surface. With a smooth surface of dough resting on the board, pull edges toward the center and pinch a seam to seal; pick up the dough and pat into an oval loaf. Smooth both ends, then tuck under and place each loaf in a 4½ by 8-inch loaf pan, greased on the bottom only. Let rise, covered, until almost doubled (about 45 minutes). Brush crusts with remaining 1 tablespoon butter. Bake in a 400° oven for 40 minutes or until loaves sound hollow when tapped. Remove loaves from pan and cool. Makes 2 loaves.

## Poppy Seed-Swirled Egg Bread

Poppy seeds, almonds, and lemon peel swirl through this bread. It is particularly good toasted.

   2 packages yeast, active dry or compressed
   ¼ cup warm (about 105°) water (lukewarm for
      compressed yeast)
   1 cup milk
   ⅓ cup butter or margarine
   ¼ cup sugar
   2 teaspoons salt
      About 5½ cups all-purpose flour, unsifted
   1 teaspoon vanilla
   4 eggs
      Poppy Seed Filling (recipe follows)
      Butter

Soften yeast in water. Scald milk; stir in butter, sugar, and salt, and cool to lukewarm. Add 2 cups of the flour; beat well. Stir in softened yeast and vanilla. Beat in eggs, 1 at a time, beating well after each addition. Stir in enough more flour to make a moderately stiff dough. Turn out on a floured board and knead until smooth and satiny. Cover and let rise in a greased bowl until doubled (about 1½ hours). Punch down, divide into 2 equal portions, and let rest 10 minutes. Roll out each half of the dough into a 6 by 18-inch rectangle; spread with half of the filling. Roll rectangle tightly into a loaf.

*(Continued on next page)*

Place loaves, seam sides down, in greased loaf pans (about 5 by 9 inches). Let rise until doubled (about 1 hour). Bake in a 375° oven for about 30 minutes or until well browned. Brush crust with butter while warm. Makes 2 loaves.

*Poppy Seed Filling.* Pour ¼ cup warm milk over ½ cup (about 2¾ oz.) poppy seed; let stand for about 1 hour. Stir in 1 tablespoon melted butter, ½ cup ground almonds, and 2 teaspoons grated lemon peel.

## Freezer Rye Bread

This dough waits in your freezer until you need it. It can be stored up to four weeks, thawed, and set to rise about 4 hours. Then you bake. The recipe makes 2 loaves. If you don't want to freeze the dough, use only 1 package of yeast and let shaped loaves rise until doubled.

1½ cups milk
¼ cup butter or margarine
½ cup firmly packed light brown sugar
2 teaspoons salt
2 packages active dry yeast
½ cup warm (about 105°) water
3 cups each *rye flour and all-purpose flour,* unsifted
1 tablespoon crushed fennel seed
Melted butter or margarine

In a pan combine the milk, butter, brown sugar, and salt; heat, stirring, until butter melts. Cool to lukewarm.

In a large bowl soften yeast in water. Stir in lukewarm milk mixture. Stir in the rye flour, 2 cups of the all-purpose flour, and fennel seed. Sprinkle about ½ cup all-purpose flour on a board and turn out dough onto floured area. Sprinkle part of the remaining ½ cup flour over dough.

With floured hands, knead until dough is smooth and not sticky (about 10 minutes), adding more flour if necessary. Divide dough in half.

*To make standard loaves*, shape each portion of dough into an oval; lift it and smooth top by pulling dough down gently and pinching a lengthwise seam underneath. Tuck ends under; pinch to seal. Place in well greased loaf pans (about 4½ by 8½ inches). Wrap and freeze immediately.

*To make round loaves*, shape each portion of dough into a round; smooth top by gently pulling dough down, and pinch to seal underneath. Place on a greased baking sheet. Cover, freeze, then wrap each loaf; return to freezer. To bake, remove loaves from freezer. Place round loaves on greased baking sheets. Cover with a cloth and let thaw at room temperature (about 2 hours). Let rise, covered, in a warm place until almost doubled (about 2 hours). Brush loaves with melted butter and bake in a 375° oven for about 30 minutes or until loaves sound hollow when tapped. Cool on racks.

## Corn-Herb Batter Bread

Batter bread bakes in coffee cans to achieve a tall, ringed shape. It produces a rich, light, moist, fine-textured bread.

1 package active dry yeast
½ cup warm (about 105°) water
2 teaspoons celery seed
1½ teaspoons ground sage
⅛ teaspoon each *marjoram leaves and ground ginger*
3 tablespoons sugar
1 can (13 oz.) undiluted evaporated milk
1 teaspoon salt
2 tablespoons salad oil
  About 4 cups all-purpose flour, unsifted
½ cup yellow cornmeal
  Butter or margarine

Dissolve yeast in water in a large mixer bowl; blend in celery seed, sage, marjoram, ginger, and 1 tablespoon of the sugar. Let stand in a warm place until mixture is bubbly (about 15 minutes). Stir in the remaining 2 tablespoons sugar and the milk, salt, and salad oil. With mixer on low speed, beat in flour 1 cup at a time, beating very well after each addition. Beat in last cup of flour and cornmeal with a heavy spoon; add flour until dough is very heavy and stiff but too sticky to knead.

Place dough in a well greased 2-pound coffee can or divide into 2 well greased 1-pound coffee cans. Cover with well greased plastic can lids. Freeze if you wish.

To bake, let covered cans stand in warm place until dough rises and pops off the plastic lids, 45 to 60 minutes for 1-pound cans, 1 to 1½ hours for

2-pound cans. (If frozen, let dough stand in cans at room temperature until lids pop; this takes 4 to 5 hours for 1-pound cans, 6 to 8 hours for 2-pound size.) Discard lids and bake in a 350° oven for 45 minutes for 1-pound cans, 60 minutes for 2-pound cans. Crust will be very brown; brush top lightly with butter.

Let cool for 5 to 10 minutes on a cooling rack, then loosen crust around edge of can with a thin knife, slide bread from can, and let cool in an upright position on rack. Makes 1 large or 2 small loaves.

## Fennel Breadsticks

Aromatic fennel seed lends an Italian flavor to these crisp tender breadsticks. They are very irregular in shape because you roll them with your fingers.

    1 package active dry yeast
    ¾ cup each warm (about 105°) water, salad
        oil, and beer
    1½ teaspoons salt
    1 tablespoon fennel seed
    4½ cups all-purpose flour, unsifted
    1 egg, beaten with 1 tablespoon water

In a large bowl, dissolve yeast in the ¾ cup warm water. Add salad oil, beer, salt, and fennel seed. With a wooden spoon, beat in 3½ cups of the flour. On a board or pastry cloth, spread remaining 1 cup flour; turn out soft dough. Knead, using this technique: lift edge of the dough, coated well with flour, and fold toward center, avoiding contact with sticky part of dough. Continue folding toward center and kneading, turning the dough as you work, until it is smooth and elastic. Place the dough in a bowl, cover, and let rise until double.

Knead air from dough. Pinch off 1½-inch diameter lumps and roll each to 18-inch long ropes. Cut each rope in half. Set cake racks on the cooky sheets and place ropes across them, ½ inch apart. Brush ropes with egg-water mixture. Bake in a 325° oven for about 35 minutes or until evenly browned. Cool, then wrap airtight and store at room temperature. Makes about 7 dozen.

## Raisin-Nut Honey Bread

Chock full of good things, this quick bread is easy to mix and nourishing to eat.

    ½ cup soft butter or margarine
    ½ cup firmly packed brown sugar
    2 eggs
    ½ cup each honey and buttermilk
    2 cups all-purpose flour, unsifted
    1 teaspoon soda
    ½ teaspoon each ground ginger and ground
        cloves
    2 teaspoons ground cinnamon
    ¼ teaspoon salt
    ½ cup each raisins and chopped walnuts

In a large mixing bowl, beat together the butter and brown sugar until smoothly blended. Add eggs, one at a time, and beat until fluffy. Blend in honey and buttermilk. Mix flour with the soda, ginger, cloves, cinnamon, and salt; mix into creamed mixture. Stir in raisins and nuts. Spoon batter into a greased 9 by 5-inch loaf pan. Bake in a 325° oven for 1 hour or until a pick inserted in center comes out clean. Cool in pan 10 minutes; turn out and cool completely. Makes 1 loaf.

## Rågbröd

Swedish Rågbröd is a sweetened rye bread flavored with honey, orange peel, fennel, and anise seed.

    2 cups milk
    2 tablespoons molasses
    ⅓ cup honey
    1½ teaspoons salt
    2 packages yeast (active dry or compressed)
    ½ cup warm (about 105°) water (lukewarm for
        compressed yeast)
    1 teaspoon each grated orange peel, crushed
        fennel seed, and crushed anise seed
    3 cups rye flour
    ¼ cup butter or margarine, melted and cooled
        to lukewarm
    5 cups all-purpose flour, unsifted
    1 egg white, slightly beaten

Scald milk and pour over molasses, honey, and salt in a large bowl. Let cool to lukewarm. Soften yeast in water; combine with milk and honey mixture. Beat in orange peel, fennel, anise, and rye flour. Blend in butter. Stir in 4½ cups of the all-purpose flour to make a soft dough. Sprinkle the last ½ cup flour onto board; turn dough onto floured board; knead until smooth (about 5 minutes). Place in greased bowl; turn dough over to grease top.

(Continued on next page)

Cover; let rise in warm place until doubled (about 1½ hours).

Punch down; divide dough in half. To shape each loaf, roll each half to make a strand 28 inches long; fold in half, then twist one half over the other twice. Place twist on lightly greased baking sheet. Cover; let rise until almost doubled (about 45 minutes). Brush with egg white. Bake in a 350° oven for 45 minutes or until a pick inserted into the center comes out clean. Makes 2 loaves.

## Rosemary Raisin Bread

Plump, round raisin bread is seasoned with rosemary and olive oil. Make it ahead to reheat or toast cold slices.

*1 package active dry yeast*
*¼ cup warm (about 105°) water*
*½ cup milk*
*3 tablespoons sugar*
*1 teaspoon each salt and rosemary leaves*
*1 whole egg*
*1 egg, separated*
*¼ cup olive oil*
*3 cups all-purpose flour, unsifted*
*½ cup raisins*
  *Olive oil*
*1 tablespoon cold water*

In a large bowl, blend the yeast with warm water; let stand about 5 minutes. Combine the milk, sugar, salt, and rosemary; heat to warm. Beat in the whole egg, egg white (save yolk for glaze), and ¼ cup olive oil, then add to yeast. Beat in the flour to blend thoroughly, then turn out onto a well floured board and knead about 10 minutes or until smooth and elastic. Flatten dough, top with raisins, and knead lightly to work raisins into dough (if some pop out, just stick them back in).

Rinse and dry the mixing bowl and coat with olive oil; place dough in bowl and invert so top surface is oiled. Cover dough and let rise in a warm place until doubled; it takes 1 to 1½ hours.

Knead dough on floured board again to expel air bubbles, then place on an olive oil-coated baking sheet and pat into a flat, 8½-inch-diameter round. Brush generously with olive oil, cover lightly, and let rise in a warm place until puffy (it takes about 30 minutes).

Slash an X across the top of the loaf with a very sharp, floured knife. Beat reserved yolk with 1 tablespoon cold water and brush over the loaf. Bake in a 350° oven for about 35 minutes or until browned. Cool slightly on a wire rack before cutting. (To reheat cold loaf, wrap in foil and place in a 350° oven for 25 minutes.) Makes 1 loaf.

## Braided Poppy Seed Coffee Cake

Each slice of this almond-studded breakfast loaf includes a thick streak of crunchy poppy seed filling; serve warm or cold.

*1 package active dry yeast*
*¼ cup warm (about 105°) water*
*¼ cup milk, scalded and cooled*
*½ teaspoon salt*
*¼ cup sugar*
*1 egg*
*¼ cup (⅛ lb.) soft butter or margarine*
  *About 3 cups all-purpose flour, unsifted*
  *Poppy Seed Filling (recipe follows)*
*1 egg white beaten with 1 teaspoon water*
*2 tablespoons sliced almonds*

In the large bowl of an electric mixer, blend yeast and water; let stand 5 minutes. Add the milk, salt, sugar, egg, butter, and 1½ cups of the flour. Blend at low speed 1 minute; turn to medium speed and beat 2 minutes, scraping sides of bowl often. With a spoon, stir in enough of remaining flour to form a soft dough.

Turn dough onto a lightly floured board and knead until smooth and elastic (about 5 minutes). Place in a greased bowl; turn dough over to grease top; cover; let rise in a warm place until almost doubled (1 to 1½ hours).

Punch down dough and turn out onto lightly floured board. With a rolling pin, roll dough into a 10 by 15-inch rectangle. Place on a lightly greased baking sheet; mark dough lightly into three lengthwise sections. Spread filling in the center third of dough. With a sharp knife, cut 10 diagonal strips in each of the two outer sections of dough, cutting in almost as far as the filling. Overlap strips; first one from one side, then one from the other, alternating until all strips are folded over.

Brush loaf with egg white mixture and sprinkle almonds evenly over top. Let rise, uncovered, in a warm place until almost doubled (about 30 minutes). Bake in a 350° oven for about 30 minutes or until richly browned. Transfer to a rack to cool. Makes 10 servings.

*Poppy Seed Filling.* In a blender jar, combine ¾ cup poppy seed and ¾ cup blanched whole almonds; whirl until mixture is the consistency of cornmeal. In a small pan, combine seed-nut mixture with ½ cup sugar, ⅓ cup milk, ¾ teaspoon grated lemon peel, 1 tablespoon lemon juice, and 3 tablespoons butter or margarine. Cook over low heat, stirring, until mixture boils and thickens (about 10 minutes). Cool.

## Swedish Cardamom Wreath

The recipe yields 2 loaves and can be made ahead, frozen if you wish, then reheated to serve.

    1 package active dry yeast
    ¼ cup warm (about 105°) water
    2½ cups milk, scalded and cooled
    ¾ cup (⅜ lb.) butter or margarine, melted and
        cooled
    1 egg
    ½ teaspoon salt
    1 cup sugar
    1½ teaspoons ground cardamom
        About 7 cups all-purpose flour, unsifted
        Sugar Icing (recipe follows)
        Red or green candied cherry, halves

In a large bowl, blend yeast and water; let stand 5 minutes. Stir in the milk, melted butter, egg, salt, sugar, and cardamon until blended.

With a heavy spoon, stir in the flour to form a stiff dough. Turn dough onto a lightly floured board and knead until smooth and elastic (about 10 minutes), adding more flour if needed. Place in a greased bowl; turn dough over to grease top; cover and let rise in a warm place until almost double (about 1½ to 2 hours).

Punch down dough and divide into 6 equal portions; then roll each to form ropes about 24 inches long. Place 3 ropes on a lightly floured board; pinch tops together and loosely braid. Form braid into a ring, pinching ends together, and place on a greased baking sheet. Repeat to make second braided wreath. Cover and let rise in a warm place until almost double (about 40 minutes).

Bake in a 350° oven for about 35 to 40 minutes or until a medium brown. If you bake both loaves in the same oven, switch their positions halfway through the baking time.

Transfer to wire racks and cool 10 minutes. Spoon sugar icing around tops of wreaths, letting it drizzle down the sides. Decorate with cherries if you wish. Or cool loaves without icing, wrap, and freeze. (To reheat, wrap each thawed loaf in foil and place in a 350° oven for about 20 minutes; then decorate with icing and cherries. Since cutting tends to squash this tender bread, it is best to pull it apart to serve.) Makes 2 large loaves.

*Sugar Icing.* For each loaf, beat until smooth 1 cup unsifted powdered sugar, 2 tablespoons milk, and ½ teaspoon lemon extract. Double recipe to make icing for 2 loaves.

## Ginger Biscuits

Crystallized ginger used generously is what distinguishes these biscuits.

    2 cups all-purpose flour, unsifted
    4 teaspoons baking powder
    ½ teaspoon salt
    ¼ cup sugar
    6 tablespoons shortening or butter
    ½ cup finely chopped crystallized ginger
        (about 3 oz.)
    2 eggs
        Milk
        About 1 tablespoon melted butter or cream

Sift together into a bowl the flour, baking powder, salt, and sugar. Cut in the shortening until it resembles small peas. Add the ginger and mix until evenly distributed. In a measuring cup beat eggs lightly, then add milk to make ½ cup liquid. Add liquid to flour mixture and stir with a fork until blended. Shape dough into a ball; on a lightly floured board, knead gently 4 or 5 times. Roll out or pat out to about ½-inch thick.

Cut with a biscuit cutter (1½ or 2 inches). Arrange on a greased baking sheet about 1½ inches apart. Brush tops lightly with the butter or cream. Bake in a 425° oven for about 10 minutes or until golden brown. Serve hot. Makes 15 large or 30 small biscuits.

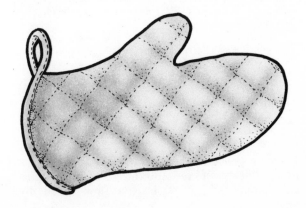

## Cinnamon Twists

Flaky Cinnamon Twists are easy to serve a number of people for brunch or breakfast. Team them up with sliced ham and fresh strawberries.

*2 packages active dry yeast*
*½ cup warm (about 105°) water*
*1 cup (½ lb.) butter or margarine*
*½ teaspoon salt*
*4 eggs*
*4 to 4½ cups all-purpose flour, unsifted*
*1 cup sugar*
*1 tablespoon ground cinnamon*

Dissolve the yeast in the warm water. In a large bowl, beat the butter and salt until creamy. Add the eggs and dissolved yeast; beat until blended. Gradually stir in enough flour so the dough cleans sides of bowl and is not sticky. Turn dough into greased bowl, cover, and refrigerate at least 2 hours or overnight.

Mix together the sugar and cinnamon. Sprinkle ½ cup of the sugar mixture on board, turn dough onto board, and knead sugar into dough just until blended. On a floured pastry cloth or well floured board, roll the dough into a rectangle 12 by 15 inches. Cut dough into strips 1 inch wide and 6 inches long. Dip strips in the remaining ½ cup sugar mixture, then, holding the ends, twist each strip. Lay on greased baking sheets and bake in a 350° oven until lightly browned (about 25 minutes). Remove from pan and serve hot or cool on racks. To reheat, place on a baking sheet and bake, uncovered, in a 350° oven for about 15 minutes. Makes about 2 dozen.

## Golden Saffron Coffee Cake

Saffron flavors as well as tints this airy coffee cake. Bake it in a 10-cup mold.

*1 package yeast, active dry or compressed*
*¼ cup warm (about 105°) water (lukewarm for compressed yeast)*
*½ cup milk, scalded and cooled to lukewarm*
*1/16 teaspoon powdered saffron*
*1 teaspoon salt*
*¼ cup sugar*
*6 eggs*
*3 cups all-purpose flour*
*½ cup (¼ lb.) butter or margarine, melted and cooled*

Dissolve yeast in the warm water in large bowl of your electric mixer. Add the cooled milk, saffron, salt, sugar, and eggs; beat at low speed until blended. Sift flour, measure, and add gradually to the milk mixture, beating until very smooth. With mixer at low speed, blend in the butter or margarine. Cover bowl lightly and let rise in a warm place about 2 hours or until doubled.

Stir dough down, then beat well. Spoon into a well-greased, 10-cup tube mold. Cover and let rise in a warm place about 30 minutes or until almost doubled. Bake in a 375° oven for 50 to 60 minutes or until golden brown. Bake until wooden pick inserted comes out clean. Let cool in pan before turning out. Makes about 12 servings.

## Breakfast Gingerbread

Spiced gingerbread goes very well with butter and orange marmalade and makes a tasty breakfast combined with eggs and ham.

*2 cups all-purpose flour, unsifted*
*1 teaspoon each baking powder, soda, and ground cinnamon*
*¼ teaspoon each salt, ground ginger, and ground cardamom*
*⅓ cup firmly packed brown sugar*
*½ cup each sour cream and molasses*
*1 egg*
*2 tablespoons melted butter or margarine*
*Powdered sugar*

Measure into a mixing bowl the flour, baking powder, soda, cinnamon, salt, ginger, cardamom, and brown sugar. Stir dry ingredients to blend well.

In another bowl, beat together the sour cream, molasses, egg, and butter. Combine wet ingredients with the dry ones and mix well. Pour batter into a greased and flour-dusted 5-cup decorative tube mold or a 5 by 9-inch loaf pan. Bake in a 350° oven for 35 to 40 minutes or until bread just begins to pull from pan sides and center springs back when lightly touched. Let stand in pan for 10 minutes, then invert gingerbread onto serving plate, dust with powdered sugar, slice thin, and serve warm. Makes 8 to 9 servings.

# Make Your Own Herb Butter

If you're a cook who likes to "season to taste," herb butters will appeal to you. When you have a meal to prepare quickly, you can add a distinctive touch by melting some flavored butter on broiled steak, fish fillets, hamburger patties, poached eggs, vegetables, French bread, or countless other items.

You add the seasonings to the butter at room temperature and whip until fluffy with an electric mixer or blender. Then store up to two weeks tightly covered in the refrigerator (or shape into a log and wrap in foil). Butter and margarine can be used interchangeably in most of these recipes, or you can use part of each.

## Fines Herbes Butter

Combine ½ cup (¼ lb.) butter or margarine, 1 tablespoon *each* minced parsley and chopped chives (fresh or freeze-dried), ½ teaspoon *each* tarragon and chervil leaves, ¼ teaspoon salt, and a dash pepper. Beat until fluffy. Cover and refrigerate.

*Suggested use.* Try on fillet of sole, hamburger patties, poached eggs, sautéed liver, and green vegetables. Spread on appetizer sandwiches or French bread.

## Garlic Butter

Combine ½ cup (¼ lb.) butter or margarine, 2 to 3 cloves garlic (minced or mashed), and 2 tablespoons minced parsley; beat until fluffy. Cover and refrigerate.

*Suggested use.* Melt on hot broiled salmon, broiled lamb chops, or beef steaks. Season boiled new potatoes, or heat on French bread slices.

## Basil Butter

Combine ½ cup (¼ lb.) butter or margarine, ½ cup lightly packed, chopped fresh basil leaves (or 2 tablespoons dried basil leaves), 2 tablespoons minced parsley, 1 tablespoon lemon juice, and ¼ cup grated Parmesan cheese in a blender. Whirl until smooth. (Or, crush basil and parsley with mortar and pestle, then beat together with other ingredients.) Cover and refrigerate.

*Suggested use.* Season minestrone and other vegetable soups; spread on tomato slices before broiling; season baked potato, zucchini, eggplant, green beans, peas, and sautéed fish.

## Mustard Butter

Combine ½ cup (¼ lb.) butter or margarine, 2 teaspoons *each* lemon juice and minced parsley, ¼ teaspoon salt, 2 tablespoons Dijon mustard, and ⅛ teaspoon pepper. Beat until fluffy. Cover and refrigerate.

*Suggested use.* Spread on bread for meat or cheese sandwiches; season asparagus, zucchini, or carrots; serve on broiled hamburgers, sautéed liver, or fish.

## Dill Butter

Press the yolks of 2 hard-cooked eggs through a wire strainer; combine with ½ cup (¼ lb.) butter or margarine, 4½ teaspoons dill weed, ½ teaspoon salt, and ⅛ teaspoon white or black pepper. Beat until fluffy. Cover and refrigerate.

*Suggested use.* Season shrimp, salmon or other fish, or poached eggs. Try it on vegetables such as new potatoes, carrots, green beans, or peas.

# Desserts

*Everything for the Sweet Tooth*

## HELPFUL HINTS

For an easy pear dessert, peel, cut in half lengthwise, and core 1 pear per serving. Arrange cut side up in greased shallow baking dish. Dot lightly with butter; dust with ground cinnamon. Cover and bake in a 400° oven for about 20 minutes (or until tender).

Jazz up a quart of lemon sherbet by softening it enough to mix in ⅓ to ½ cup finely chopped candied ginger. Refreeze.

To present fresh strawberries a new way, mix 2 tablespoons brown sugar and ½ teaspoon ground cinnamon on a plate. Turn 1 large package (8 oz.) cream cheese at room temperature in sugar mixture, coating all sides. Place on a serving tray with 2 boxes unhulled strawberries and 2 dozen hard, mildly sweet cookies such as Petit Beurre butter biscuits. Use it to spread on cookies or as a dip for berries.

Slices of melon are enhanced by just a sprinkling of ground ginger before serving.

Store a vanilla bean in an airtight container with granulated sugar, brown sugar, or powdered sugar for at least a week. It will give a vanilla flavor to cakes, cookies, and one-crust pies when sugar is sprinkled over top or used in the baking.

## Gravenstein Apple Pie with Variations

It's an adventure to try pies flavored with faintly exotic seasonings. We give you three different pies to try.

Pastry for a 9-inch double crust pie
About 3 pounds or 7 medium-sized
   Gravenstein apples, peeled and cored
¾ cup sugar
¼ cup all-purpose flour or 3 tablespoons quick-
   cooking tapioca or 2½ tablespoons cornstarch
1 teaspoon ground cinnamon
¼ teaspoon ground cardamom or ground ginger
2 tablespoons butter or margarine

On a floured pastry cloth or board, roll out half of the pastry into a circle about ⅛ inch thick; fit pastry into a 9-inch pie pan and trim off excess even with the pan rim. Roll out remaining pastry into a 13-inch circle. Cover with a damp towel while preparing apples.

Cut apples into 1¼-inch-thick slices and measure 8 cups, packed compactly without crushing. In a large bowl, stir together the sugar, flour (or tapioca or cornstarch), cinnamon, and cardamom. Add the apple slices and mix lightly to coat. Mound apples into the pastry-lined pan. Dot top with butter.

Fit pastry over apples, extending a 1-inch border over edge; trim away excess. Tuck border under edge of bottom pastry and crimp decoratively between your fingers or press edge with a fork to seal edge around pie. Cut vents in top pastry.

Bake pie in a 400° oven for 50 to 60 minutes or until pastry is well browned and juices inside pie bubble vigorously. If pastry edges begin to brown too much, cover edge with a strip of foil. Cool pan on a wire rack for at least 30 minutes before serving. Serve warm. To reheat, place pie in a 350° oven for about 15 minutes.

To serve, cut wedges of slightly cooled or reheated pie; present unadorned or accompany with a scoop of ice cream for pie à la mode or with a slice of sharp Cheddar cheese.

*Apple Pie with Fennel*

Follow traditional apple pie recipe, omitting cinnamon. Instead use 1½ teaspoons fennel seed or anise seed. Measure seed, then crush thoroughly before mixing with the sugar.

*Apple Pie with Chinese Five-Spice*

Follow traditional apple pie recipe, omitting cinnamon and cardamom; instead use 1½ teaspoons Chinese five-spice (or ½ teaspoon *each* ground ginger and cinnamon, ¼ teaspoon *each* ground allspice and crushed anise seed, and ⅛ teaspoon cloves).

## Pumpkin Chiffon Pie

A ginger cooky crust provides tangy contrast for this light pumpkin chiffon that requires no baking. You can use pumpkin pie spice or Chinese five-spice as a choice of seasonings.

Ginger Cooky Crumb Crust (recipe, page 74)
1 envelope unflavored gelatin
¾ cup firmly packed brown sugar
¼ teaspoon salt
1½ teaspoons pumpkin pie spice or 1 teaspoon
   Chinese five-spice
3 eggs, separated
½ cup milk
¼ cup water
1½ cups canned pumpkin
⅓ cup granulated sugar
   Whipped cream (optional)

Prepare the crumb crust and set in refrigerator. Combine the gelatin, brown sugar, salt, and pumpkin spice or Chinese five-spice in a saucepan. Beat egg yolks slightly and stir in milk, water, and pumpkin; add to sugar mixture. Cook over medium heat, stirring constantly, to just below simmering point. Set pan in ice water (or refrigerate); stir occasionally until mixture is cold and slightly thickened.

*(Continued on next page)*

In a bowl, beat egg whites until thick; add granulated sugar, about 1 tablespoon at a time, and beat well after each addition. Beat until whites hold firm peaks. Fold gelatin mixture into the beaten egg whites. Pour into prepared pie shell and chill at least 4 hours or overnight. Serve with a spoonful of sweetened whipped cream on each piece, if you wish. Makes a 9-inch pie.

*Ginger Cooky Crumb Crust.* Combine 1¼ cups fine gingersnap cooky crumbs with 3 tablespoons sifted powdered sugar. Stir in 3 tablespoons melted butter. Press lightly into the bottom and sides of 9-inch pie pan.

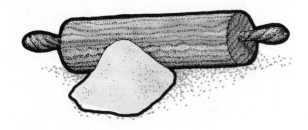

## Ginger Pear Pie

Soft and billowy meringue tops this almond-accented fruit pie.

> Pastry for single-crust 9-inch pie
> 1 can (1 lb. 13 oz.) pear halves, well drained
> 3 eggs, separated
> ⅓ cup milk
> ½ cup firmly packed brown sugar
> ½ teaspoon ground ginger
> ¼ teaspoon almond extract
> 1 tablespoon lemon juice
> 6 tablespoons sugar

Prepare your favorite pastry or use a pie crust mix. Roll out on a lightly floured board to fit into a 9-inch pie pan; flute edge. Arrange pear halves, cut side down, in pastry shell.

Beat egg yolks slightly, then beat in milk, brown sugar, ginger, almond extract, and lemon juice; pour over pears. Bake in a 400° oven for 25 minutes or until custard mixture is set. Remove pie from oven and cool slightly; reset the oven temperature to 350°.

With an electric mixer at highest speed, beat egg whites until frothy; add sugar gradually (about 1 tablespoon every 30 seconds). Continue beating until soft peaks form. Swirl over pie, touching meringue to crust to completely enclose filling. Bake in a 350° oven for 20 minutes or until golden. Makes 6 servings.

## Vanilla Bean Custard

French cooks traditionally bake and serve rich custard in small individual containers called *pots de crème* (pronounced po d'crem). If you do not have the little pots, you can use demitasse cups or any other small, heat-resistant ceramic or porcelain containers and cover them with lids or pieces of foil.

> 2 cups half-and-half (light cream)
> ½ cup sugar
> 1 vanilla bean
> Few grains salt
> 6 egg yolks, slightly beaten

Combine the half-and-half, sugar, vanilla bean, and salt in a pan or double boiler; heat to scalding, stirring over medium heat or over boiling water. Remove from heat and let stand until cool (about 30 minutes). Remove the vanilla bean and reheat the cream to scalding. Slowly beat the hot cream into the beaten egg yolks. Strain into 6 individual cups, cover with lids or foil, set the cups in a baking pan, and pour boiling water into the pan to a depth of about 1 inch. Bake in a 350° oven 20 to 40 minutes. Quickly uncover cups and cool. Makes 6 servings.

## Spicy Molasses Pudding

Pour warm Lemon Sauce over squares of this spicy pudding, warm or cooled. Or you can top it with whipped cream instead.

> 2½ cups all-purpose flour, unsifted
> ¾ cup sugar
> 1 teaspoon ground nutmeg
> 1½ teaspoons ground cinnamon
> ½ teaspoon each ground ginger and salt
> 1 teaspoon soda
> ½ cup (¼ lb.) butter or margarine
> ½ cup chopped walnuts or almonds
> ¾ cup molasses
> 1 cup water
> Lemon Sauce (recipe follows)

Sift together into a bowl the flour, sugar, nutmeg, cinnamon, ginger, salt, and soda. Using a pastry blender or two knives, cut butter into flour mixture until mixture reaches the consistency of coarse crumbs. Stir in nuts.

Combine the molasses and water; pour into flour mixture and stir just until blended. Pour into a greased, 9-inch-square baking pan. Bake in a 350° oven for 50 minutes or until an inserted pick comes out clean. Makes 9 servings.

*Lemon Sauce.* In a pan, combine 4 teaspoons cornstarch, ¼ cup sugar, and a dash salt. Stir in 1 cup water; cook, stirring, until thickened. Remove from heat and stir in 1 teaspoon grated lemon peel and 3 tablespoons each lemon juice and butter. Serve warm.

## Peach Cardamom Delight

Spiced peaches make a sumptuous, easy-to-make topping for vanilla ice cream.

*1 can (about 1 lb.) sliced cling peaches*
*½ teaspoon ground cardamom*
*1 teaspoon grated lemon peel*
   *Vanilla ice cream*
   *Whipped cream (optional)*

Drain the syrup from the peaches into a saucepan. Turn peaches into a bowl. Bring syrup to boiling; boil a few minutes to reduce and thicken slightly. Remove from heat; stir in the cardamom and lemon peel; pour over peaches. Chill. Spoon over ice cream; top each serving with whipped cream, if you wish. Makes 6 servings.

## Old-Fashioned Spice Cake

Use your favorite caramel or butterscotch frosting (or prepared frosting mix) to fill between the layers of this cake.

*¾ cup (⅜ lb.) butter or margarine*
*1½ cups sugar*
*3 eggs, separated*
*¾ cup buttermilk*
*2 cups all-purpose flour*
*2 teaspoons cocoa*
*¾ teaspoons each ground nutmeg, soda, and*
   *baking powder*
*1 teaspoon ground cinnamon*
*½ teaspoon lemon extract*
*1 teaspoon vanilla*
*½ cup chopped dates*
*1 cup chopped walnuts*

Cream butter or margarine with sugar until light. Mix in egg yolks and buttermilk. Sift flour, measure, and sift again with cocoa, nutmeg, soda, baking powder, and cinnamon, adding gradually to creamed mixture. Beat until well blended. Stir in lemon extract, vanilla, dates, and nuts.

Beat egg whites until stiff but not dry; fold into batter. Turn into two buttered, 9-inch layer cake pans. Bake in a 375° oven for 25 to 30 minutes or until done. Makes 10 to 12 servings.

## Poppy Seed Cake

A whole package of poppy seed gives a crunchy texture.

*1 package (about 1 lb. 3 oz.) yellow butter*
   *cake mix*
*1 package (⅓ to ⅔ cup) poppy seed*
*¼ cup (⅛ lb.) butter or margarine*
*⅓ cup milk*
*1 cup firmly packed brown sugar*
*1½ to 2 cups sifted powdered sugar*

Prepare the cake mix as directed, adding the ingredients called for on the package. Fold in the poppy seed after final beating. Pour batter into two greased, 9-inch layer cake pans or into a greased, 9 by 13-inch loaf pan. Bake as directed on the package. Cool cake layers on racks before frosting. Or cool loaf cake in the pan.

For the frosting, combine in a small saucepan the butter, milk, and brown sugar. Bring to a full boil, stirring constantly. Boil over medium heat for 1 minute. Remove from heat and cool to lukewarm. Beat in the powdered sugar to make a good spreading consistency. Spread between the layers and on tops and sides of layer cake; spread only on top of loaf cake. Makes about 12 servings.

## Caraway Pound Cake

You can slice this cake thinly or cut in thicker slices to spread with butter, then lightly toast.

*1 package (about 1 lb. 1 oz.) pound cake mix*
*1 teaspoon finely grated orange peel*
*¼ teaspoon ground mace or nutmeg*
*½ cup finely chopped pecans or almonds*
*2 to 4 teaspoons caraway seed*
   *Powdered sugar (optional)*

Prepare the cake mix as directed, adding the ingredients called for on the package. In addition, beat in the orange peel and mace. After beating, fold in the pecans and caraway seed. Pour into a greased, 5 by 9-inch loaf pan and bake as directed.

Cool the cake about 10 minutes, then turn out of pan and cool completely. At serving time, sift powdered sugar over the cake, if you wish. Makes about 10 servings.

## Crisp Nutmeg Cookies

Chill the dough thoroughly before rolling. Then cut out shapes with your favorite cooky cutter.

    1 cup (½ lb.) soft butter
    1 cup sugar
    1 egg
 3½ cups all-purpose flour
    ⅛ teaspoon salt
    1 teaspoon each ground nutmeg and soda
    ½ cup buttermilk

Cream the butter until light and fluffy. Gradually beat in the sugar and egg. Sift flour; measure and sift again with the salt, nutmeg, and soda. Add to the creamed mixture alternately with the buttermilk. Shape the dough into a ball and chill

several hours until firm. Roll out a small portion of dough at a time on a well-floured board until very thin (keep rest of dough in refrigerator). Cut with cooky cutters. Bake on an ungreased baking sheet in a 350° oven for 10 minutes or until lightly browned. Makes about 6 dozen cookies.

## Ginger Oatmeal Cookies

Ginger and oats blend in these chewy-crisp cookies. They will stay fresh for up to two weeks when stored airtight.

 ¾ cup (⅜ lb.) butter or margarine
    1 cup sugar
    1 egg
    ¼ cup light molasses
 1½ cups all-purpose flour, unsifted
    2 teaspoons soda
    ½ teaspoon salt
    1 teaspoon ground cinnamon
    ¾ teaspoon each ground cloves and ground
        ginger
    2 cups regular or quick-cooking rolled oats

In a bowl, beat together the butter and sugar until creamy; beat in the egg and molasses until

## Making an Herbal Tea

Shades of mysticism may come to mind when herbal tea is mentioned. Until recently, herbal teas were not common in the American culture even though they have been enjoyed in many foreign societies for centuries.

An herbal tea is one made from either dried herbs, fresh chopped herbs, or crushed seeds. They can be made by pouring boiling water over the herbs and letting them steep until the desired strength has been reached (usually at least 10 minutes). Be willing to experiment to find the right flavors and strengths for your personal liking. Begin by trying about 1 teaspoon of dried herbs or crushed seed for each 6 ounce serving. Use about 3 times as much if using fresh herbs. You can either put the herb directly into the teapot or into a tea ball.

If you like your tea a little sweeter, try some sugar or honey. You might also like lemon in your tea, but all herbed teas are best without cream or milk.

All tastes differ, but it's fun to experiment and try the teas on your guests to get their reaction too. Some herbs to start with are bay leaves, mint leaves, thyme leaves, rosemary leaves, parsley, marjoram leaves, anise seed, sage leaves, or savory leaves.

smooth. Stir together the flour, soda, salt, cinnamon, cloves, and ginger. Stir into the butter mixture until blended. Stir in the rolled oats. Drop by level tablespoonfuls on lightly greased cooky sheets, placing dough about 3 inches apart. Bake in a 350° oven for about 8 minutes or until browned. Cool for about 1 minute on the pan, then remove and cool completely on wire racks. Makes about 4 dozen.

## Clove Cookies

These crisp butter cookies spiced with ground cloves can survive the adventurous trip to school in a sack or lunch-box.

½ cup (¼ lb.) melted butter or margarine
1 cup sugar
1 teaspoon vanilla
1 egg
1 cup all-purpose flour, unsifted
1 teaspoon ground cloves

Stir melted butter into the sugar until blended; stir in vanilla. Beat in the egg until smooth. Stir the flour and cloves together, then stir into the butter mixture until blended.

Drop batter by level teaspoonfuls on a lightly greased cooky sheet, placing dough about 2 inches apart. Bake in a 350° oven for 12 minutes or until edges are golden brown and puffy tops start to crinkle and collapse. Let cool on the pan for about 30 seconds, then transfer cookies to wire rack to cool completely. Makes about 4 dozen.

## Vanilla Butter Wafers

Cookies are sandwiched together with smooth, uncooked butter cream filling.

1 cup (½ lb.) butter
2 cups all-purpose flour, unsifted
⅓ cup whipping cream
  Sugar
  Vanilla Cream (recipe follows)

Cut the butter into the flour until particles are no larger than small peas. Stir in the whipping cream with a fork until mixture holds together. Shape dough into a ball and divide in thirds. Chill two portions while you roll out a third on a well sugared board until dough is ⅛ inch thick; turn dough several times and use enough sugar to prevent sticking. Cut in 1-inch diameter rounds and space slightly apart on ungreased baking sheet.

Chill the scraps of dough. Prick each round several times with a fork. Repeat this procedure with remaining portions of dough, one at a time. Shape scraps into a ball and roll out on a board that has a little flour mixed with the sugar; cut and prick.

Bake in a 375° oven for about 10 minutes or until a pale golden brown. Let cool on baking sheet, then remove gently. To fill cookies, spread one with some of the Vanilla Cream and top with another cooky; repeat until all are filled. Store in refrigerator, wrapped airtight, for as long as a week, or freeze. Makes about 5½ dozen sandwich cookies.

*Vanilla Cream.* Cream ¼ cup (⅛ lb.) soft butter with 1½ cups sifted powdered sugar, 1 egg yolk, and 1 teaspoon vanilla until smooth and easy to spread.

## Twice-Baked Italian Cookies

First you shape the dough into loaves and bake until firm, then you cut the loaves in thick slices and bake cookies again until they develop a mild toasted flavor. These hard, anise-flavored cookies keep very well.

2 cups sugar
1 cup (½ lb.) butter, melted
4 tablespoons anise seed
4 tablespoons anise-flavored liqueur
3 tablespoons bourbon, or 2 teaspoons vanilla
    and 2 tablespoons water
2 cups coarsely chopped almonds or walnuts
6 eggs
5½ cups all-purpose flour
1 tablespoon baking powder

Mix sugar with butter, anise seed, anise liqueur, bourbon, and nuts. Beat in the eggs. Sift the flour, then measure and sift again with baking powder into the sugar mixture; blend thoroughly. Cover and chill the dough for 2 to 3 hours.

(Continued on next page)

On a lightly floured board, shape dough with your hands to form flat loaves that are about ½ inch thick, 2 inches wide, and as long as your cooky sheets. Place no more than 2 loaves, parallel and well apart, on a buttered cooky sheet (one without rim is best). Bake in a 375° oven for 20 minutes.

Remove from oven and let loaves cool on pans until you can touch them, then cut in diagonal slices that are about ½ to ¾ inch thick. Lay slices on cut sides close together on cooky sheet and return to the oven for 15 minutes more or until lightly toasted. Cool on wire racks and store in airtight containers. Makes about 9 dozen.

# Spice Up Your Coffee

Several simple additions can make pleasing changes in a cup of coffee. Usually the spices that tend to sweeten are most effective.

**Cardamom Coffee** is easily made by cracking a pod of whole cardamom between your fingers and dropping it into each regular sized cup. Fill with hot coffee and serve.

**Café Brûlot** is a bit more dramatic when presented. Put the peel of 1 orange, cut in a spiral, into an attractive, heat-proof punch bowl. Add 2 sticks whole cinnamon (each 3 inches long), 20 whole cloves, 1 cup warmed brandy or Cognac, and 14 lumps of sugar. Bring to table; tip bowl and touch lighted match to edge of liquid to set aflame. Use a ladle to stir the mixture constantly while it burns (about 2 minutes). Slowly pour in 1⅔ cups hot, strong coffee. Ladle at once into after-dinner-sized demitasse cups. Makes 8 small cups coffee.

**Quick Café au Lait** just requires heating 1 cup milk to simmering for each serving and stirring in 1 tablespoon instant coffee, 1 teaspoon sugar, and dash ground cinnamon.

**Mocha Marbled Coffee,** on the other hand, becomes more like a dessert in itself. Whip 1 cup whipping cream until stiff and blend with ¼ cup sugar and 1 teaspoon vanilla. Fold in 2 ounces chopped or coarsely grated semi-sweet chocolate. Fill regular-sized cups with hot coffee and top each with 2 or 3 tablespoons of the flavored whipped cream. Sprinkle each with a little more chopped semi-sweet chocolate, if you like. Topping is enough for 8 to 10 servings.

**Viennese Coffee** is brewed extra strength, then poured into regular-sized cups and topped with a dollop of sweetened whipped cream. Dust the cream with ground nutmeg or cinnamon.

# Index